Spanish in 32 Lessons

By Adrienne

French in 32 Lessons
German in 32 Lessons
Spanish in 32 Lessons
Italian in 32 Lessons

The Gimmick Series for the more advanced student

Français parlé
gesprochenes Deutsch
Español hablado
Italiano parlato

The Gimmick Series
Spanish in 32 Lessons

Adrienne

W · W · NORTON & COMPANY

New York · London

Copyright © 1979 by Adrienne Penner

Reissued as a Norton paperback 1995

Printed in the United States of America

Adapted from the French edition published by Flammarion 1977
© Flammarion 1977

Library of Congress Cataloging-in-Publication Data
Adrienne,
    Spanish in 32 lessons.
    (The Gimmick series)
    British ed. (1978) has title: Spanish in no time.
    1. Spanish language—Grammar—1950–   2. Spanish
language—Conversation and phrase books.   3. Spanish
language—Self-instruction.   I. Title.
PC4112.A3   1979   468´.3´421   79-2048

ISBN 0-393-31305-0

W. W. Norton & Company, Inc., 500 Fifth Avenue, New York, N.Y. 10110
W. W. Norton & Company Ltd., 10 Coptic Street, London WC1A 1PU

    4 5 6 7 8 9 0

For Carolyn and Jimmy McGown
and their grandfather

I am very grateful for the collaboration of Catherine Rusquet

Contents/Contenido

Preface/Prefacio

Lección 1   1
¿QUÉ ES ESO? (What is it?)
—ES UN . . .

Lección 2   4
¿QUÉ ES ESO? (What are they?)
—SON . . .
Opuestos (opposites) 1

Lección 3   11
POSSESSIVE ADJECTIVES AND PRONOUNS
—MI, MÍO
¿DE QUIÉN?

Lección 4   16
POSSESSION
¿QUÉ HORA ES? (What time is it?)
¿QUÉ? (What? Which?)

Lección 5   19
SER — ESTAR (TO BE)
—ES (it's)
TAMBIÉN ≠ TAMPOCO (also ≠ either)
Opuestes 2

Lección 6   26
ESTE ≠ ESTA (this ≠ that)
HAY (there is/there are)
¿CUÁNTO(S)? (how many?)
Adverbios y frases (adverbs and phrases) 1

Lección 7   31
TIEMPO PRESENTE (present tense)
—verbs in AR
PERSONAL A
special negatives

Lección 8   38
TIEMPO PRESENTE
–verbs in ER
special negatives

Lección 9   42
TENER (to have)
ALGUNOS = UNOS (some)
TO HAVE TO/MUST (present)
—Adverbios y frases 2

Lección 10   47
TIEMPO PRESENTE
—verbs in IR
special negatives

Lección 11   51
DIRECT OBJECT PRONOUNS
—¿QUÉ? QUIÉN? (who? whom?)
—YO — ME (I → me)

Lección 12   56
INDIRECT OBJECT PRONOUNS
—YO — ME (A MÍ)
—attached pronouns

Lección 13   61
¿QUIÉN? ¿QUÉ? QUE (who? what? that)
NUNCA (never, ever)
CONOCER — SABER (to know)
Opuestas 3

Lección 14   66
PRESENT PARTICIPLE (—ING)
—ESTAR + ANDO

Lección 15   70
PUBLIC ENEMY NUMBER ONE:
I've been working for . . .
—¿HACE CUÁNTO TIEMPO QUE   . . (for how long)
—DESDE (since), DESDE HACE (for)
Adverbios y frases 3

Lección 16   75
TIEMPO FUTURO (future)

Lección 17   79
SI = IF (conditional 1)
—Opuestas 4

Lección 18   82
THE COMPARATIVE FORM
TANTO . . . COMO (as . . . as)
ADVERB = ADJECTIVE + 'MENTE'
ALGUIEN ≠ NADIE (someone ≠ no one)
ALGO ≠ NADA (something ≠ anything)

Lección 19   88
PRETÉRITO (past — specific time)
special negatives

Lección 20   96
IMPERFECTO (past — duration of time — WAS + —ING)

Lección 21
CONDICIONAL + sequence of tenses   101

Lección 22   106
SI = IF (conditional 2)

Lección 23   110
PRETÉRITO INDEFINIDO (indefinite past) = PRESENT PERFECT
—HE HABLADO (I have spoken)
—YA (already) ≠ NO TODAVÍA/AÚN (not yet)

Lección 24   116
VOY A (I'm going to)
ACABAR DE (to have just)
TODAVIA (still) ≠ NO MAS = YA NO (no more)
¿LE GUSTA? (do you like?)
Averbios y frases 4

Lección 25   122
LO QUE (what)
ESTAR ACOSTUMBRADO A — SOLER (to be used to)
CUYO (whose)
HACER FALTA (to need)
Adverbios y frases 5

Lección 26   128
SI = IF (conditional 3)

Lección 27   134
TENER QUE — HAY QUE — DEBER (must/have to)

Lección 28   138
TAN QUE (so)
TANTO (so much)
¿QUE TE PARECE? (What do you think?)
PERO, SINO (but)

Lección 29   142
AÚN MÁS — TODAVÍA MÁS (still more)
HABRÁ (there will be)
HABÍA (there were)
VOLVER A (to do again)
APOCOPATION — primero → primer

Lección 30
VERBOS REFLEXIVOS (reflexive verbs) — present   146
ME LAVO (I'm getting washed)

Lección 31   150
YO MISMO (myself)
verbos reflexivos — past   153

Lección 32
VERB REVISION

VERBOS Y PREPOSICIONES (verbs and prepositions)   161
THE CASE OF THE MISSING PREPOSITIONS, ETC.   167
MODISMOS (idioms)   168

KEY   177

Preface/Prefacio

The Gimmicks for the more advanced student have been found so useful by
so many — in French, German, Spanish and English — throughout Europe
and America — that I have prepared a method to meet the needs of students
at an earlier stage of language learning. There is much to criticize in present
methods.

Beginners aren't imbeciles!
The boring repetition of inane exercises in 'modern' methods is an insult to
the intelligence. To repeat, endlessly, structured sentences is a sure way to
kill the discovery of one's own style. Without the freedom to make mistakes,
the student will never learn to 'feel' the language. This is why, after a year or
more of study, the student, often, can barely get a sentence out on his own.
Emphasis on constant structuring discourages creativity, and speaking a
language is a creative process.

Forced feeding
It's no good having perfect grammar if your vocabulary is limited to a few
words. This is THE problem in language learning, for a language IS ITS
VOCABULARY. Grammar and writing exercises over and over should not
be dwelt on ridiculously. It will come automatically if vocabulary is learned
properly. It doesn't matter if the beginner is lost . . . confused. Beginners are
not fragile. They won't break. I don't ask mine to understand. I ask them to
learn . . . hundreds of words. The theorist may need high grammar. Mr and
Ms John Q. Public need words in order to understand and be understood.
Vocabulary should be programmed and progressive — and gobbled up.

Tests
TESTS ARE ABSOLUTELY INDISPENSABLE FOR THOSE WHO WANT
TO LEARN A LANGUAGE IN LESS THAN TEN YEARS! You can be
tested by the teacher or by a friend. Each lesson should be well tested,
written if possible, to make sure the words are 'in the head' and not just in
the book. And, as learning is rarely 'solid' the first time, the same test should
be repeated throughout the year. You must memorize hundreds, thousands
of words. There is no way to communicate without words. I don't care how
perfect your grammar is.

Mistakes are an asset!
Making mistakes is one of the principal ways the student learns a language . . .
when it really sinks in. For verbs there is nothing better. Written resumés are

excellent for this reason, and the student should write them for homework as of the first lesson: at first a small paragraph about his house, job, family, etc., and then a page summary of a movie, etc. This is the way he will find his style.

Homework
Homework is always a good thing — if only studying for constant vocabulary tests. Written summaries are an excellent way to ensure that verbs and vocabulary are being assimilated.

Pace
A very good class can assimilate one lesson a week (a once- or twice-a-week class). Those with less time might need two to three weeks for each lesson.

Not stictly kosher!
When necessary to facilitate learning, I have sacrificed strict grammatical explanations. The purist may frown on this, but the student will understand more easily. As it is easier to learn a group of words rather than the classic one-to-one translation, the vocabulary is taught by association.

Institut audio-visuel
Those who want to contact me personally should write to: Adrienne, IAV, 40 rue de Berri, 75008 Paris, France.

The ideal lesson
An ideal lesson might include:
— 15 minutes: the students ask each other questions to begin the class — using the verbs and vocabulary they have learned.
— 20 minutes: oral summary of a story, film, etc.
— 15 minutes: test (written and corrected).
— 15 minutes: grammar drills and vocabulary explanation from book, etc.
—20 minutes: read story or article — and give quick summaries.

Optional
— 10 minutes: dictation.
— 20 minutes: debate.
— 20 minutes: scene playing.

Spanish in 32 Lessons

BOXED IN!

The 'boxes' are there to concentrate your attention on the vital basic skeleton of language. Read and assimilate each well. Then learn the vocabulary by heart, always testing yourself by writing it down. Next do the exercises, correcting your work with the key at the end of the book. Each lesson represents about one week's work. After years and years of teaching executives, journalists, actors, ministers and diplomats — this method works! This is the best class text or 'self-learner' in town!!

LECCIÓN 1

¿ES UN COCHE NEGRO?	Is it a black car?
Sí, es un coche negro.	Yes, it's a black car.
No, no es un coche negro.	No, it isn't a black car.

¿QUÉ ES ESO?	What is it?
Es un coche negro.	It's a black car.

learn the numbers:

0 = **cero**   1 = **uno**   2 = **dos**   3 = **tres**   4 = **cuatro**   5 = **cinco**

translate:

1) Is it a big table?
2) It isn't a black door.
3) See you soon.
4) Is it a little dog?
5) Darn it!
6) It isn't a big black book, but a big blue book.
7) What is it? It's a watch.
8) Is it a red telephone?
9) It isn't a little chair.
10) Is it a white alarm-clock?
11) Is it a blue wall?
12) It isn't a mouse.
13) Is it a black pencil?
14) It isn't a big cat.

```
UN = A (masculine              UNA = A (feminine)

    hombre = a man                 mujer = a woman
un  libro = a book          una    silla = a chair
```

note: Words in Spanish are either masculine (frequently ending in 'o'), or feminine (frequently ending in 'a'); there are a few exceptions to the o/a rule, e.g. la mano = hand; el día = day.

```
ADJECTIVES

un libro blanco              una silla blanca
a white book                 a white chair
```

note: The adjective usually follows the noun.

give the affirmative and negative answers:

1) ¿Es un gato pequeño?
2) ¿Es un perro blanco?
3) ¿Es un teléfono azul?
4) ¿Es una pared blanca?
5) ¿Es un libro negro?
6) ¿Es un bolígrafo?
7) ¿Es un reloj azul marino?
8) ¿Es un lápiz negro?
9) ¿Es una silla roja?
10) ¿Es un papel?
11) ¿Es un ratón blanco?
12) ¿Es una puerta?
13) ¿Es un despertador pequeño?
14) ¿Es una mesa grande?

2

VOCABULARIO = VOCABULARY

	traducción = translation	sinónimo asociado = associated synonym	opuesto asociado = associated opposite
1. (el) gato	cat	(el) ratón = mouse	(el) perro = dog
2. (la) mesa	table ≠ chair		(la) silla
3. sí	yes ≠ no		no
4. hola	hello ≠ goodbye		adiós
5. otra vez	again	de nuevo	
6. (la) pared	wall	(el) muro	
7. (el) teléfono	telephone		
8. (el) bolígrafo	ball-point pen	(la) tinta = ink	(el) lápiz = pencil
9. (el) reloj	/watch/clock	(el) despertador = alarm-clock	
10. (la) puerta	door		
11. /y/o	/and/or	note: y → e before i and hi; o → u before o and ho	
12. negro	black ≠ white		blanco
13. jolín!	darn it!	¡caramba! ¡mierda! = ¡shit! = ¡joder! – ¡coño!	
14. pequeño	little ≠ big		grande
15. /el, la (los, las)/un (una)	/the/a, an		
16. rojo	red	rosa = pink	
17. azul	blue	azul marino = navy	
18. (el) libro	book	(el) papel = paper	
19. (los) deberes	homework		
20. hasta pronto	see you soon	hasta la vista, hasta luego, hasta entonces	

LECCIÓN 2

¿SON CIGARRILLOS LARGOS?	Are they long cigarettes?
Sí, son cigarrillos largos.	Yes, they're long cigarettes.
No, no son cigarrillos largos.	No, they aren't long cigarettes.

note: — un, una = a (singular)
      — unos, unas = some (plural)
      — adjectives (except those of quantity: mucho = much, a lot of; poco = few, bastante = enough, algunos = some) are usually placed after the noun.

¿QUÉ ES ESO?	What are they?
Son cigarrillos largos.	They're long cigarettes.

translate:

1) How are you? Fine, thank you, and you?
2) Are they strong cigarettes?
3) Are they brown coats?
4) I'm sorry, I apologize.
5) Are the streets wide?
6) Time's up.
7) The gals are young and thin.
8) That's it.
9) The guys are rich, but the kids are poor.
10) Could you repeat it, please?

note: Each lesson should begin with a drill of the previous lessons and a quick written test.

SINGULAR	→ PLURAL
un libro blanco a white book	**unos** libros blancos some white books
una chica rica a rich girl	**unas** chicas ricas some rich girls

note: — the plural of a noun or adjective is formed by adding 's'
— if the noun is plural, the adjective is also plural
— if the word ends in a consonant, add '**es**': mujer → mujeres (women), azul → azules (blue), fácil → fáciles (easy)
— adjectives ending in '**z**' change the ending to '**ces**': feliz → felices (happy)

un/el libro blanco	— **un/el**	= article
	— **libro**	= noun
	— **blanco**	= adjective

learn the numbers:

6 = **seis**   7 = **siete**   8 = **ocho**   9 = **nueve**   10 = **diez**

put in the plural:

1) un tío débil
2) una mujer pequeña
3) un niño fuerte
4) un calcetín marrón
5) un abrigo largo
6) un cenicero bonito
7) un mechero corto
8) una tarde mala
9) un reloj viejo
10) una niña grande

11) una calle estrecha
12) un papel grueso
13) un sombrero azul
14) un libro rojo
15) una llave grande
16) una caja verde
17) un chico feliz
18) una cerilla larga
19) una lección fácil
20) un perro blanco

5

```
┌─────────────────────────────────────────────────────────────┐
│  EL/LOS — LA/LAS              =  THE                          │
│  el libro = the book          los libros = the books         │
│  la silla = the chair         las sillas = the chairs        │
└─────────────────────────────────────────────────────────────┘
```

```
┌─────────────────────────────────────────────────────────────┐
│  ¿EL GATO      BLANCO?        Is the cat white?               │
│             ES                                                │
│  ¿LA GATA      BLANCA?                                        │
│                                                               │
│  Sí, el gato/la gata es blanco(a)    Yes, the cat's white.    │
│  No, el gato/la gata no es blanco(a) No, the cat isn't white. │
└─────────────────────────────────────────────────────────────┘
```

note: — el gato = male cat; la gata = female cat
      — usually the intonation of the voice tells you that it's a question.
       However, you can also say: ¿Es blanco el gato?

give the singular and plural negative answers:

e.g. ¿Es negro el gato?
    — No, el gato no es negro.
    — No, los gatos no son negros.

1)	¿Es grande la mujer?	15)	¿Es pesada la primera puerta?
2)	¿Es débil el hombre?	16)	¿Es larga la última lección?
3)	¿Es gordo el libro?	17)	¿Es negra la llave?
4)	¿Es pequeño el cuarto?	18)	¿Es azul el abrigo?
5)	¿Es interesante la lección?	19)	¿Es malo el perro?
6)	¿Es liviana la mesa?	20)	¿Es delgada la chica?
7)	¿Es pequeño el zapato?		
8)	¿Es gordo el niño?		
9)	¿Es joven la chica?		
10)	¿Es ancho el zapato?		
11)	¿Es fino el papel?		
12)	¿Es rico el tío?		
13)	¿Es ancha la calle?		
14)	¿Es viejo el perro?		

translate and answer in the negative, singular and plural:
e.g. ¿Son tíos interesantes?
   — No, no son tíos interesantes.
   ⊥ No, no es un tío interesante.

1) ¿Son relojes azules?
2) ¿Son hombres gordos?
3) ¿Son mujeres felices?
4) ¿Son cajas amarillas?
5) ¿Son zapatos grandes?
6) ¿Son calles estrechas?
7) ¿Son niños bonitos?
8) ¿Son impermeables largos?
9) ¿Son sombreros rojos?
10) ¿Son cuartos viejos?
11) ¿Son gatos negros?
12) ¿Son tíos fuertes?
13) ¿Son las últimas lecciones?
14) ¿Son chicos ricos?
15) ¿Son perros gordos?
16) ¿Son zapatos azul marino?
17) ¿Son cigarrillos malos?
18) ¿Son sombreros verdes?
19) ¿Son llaves pequeñas?
20) ¿Son ratones blancos?

translate and put in the interrogative form, singular and plural:
e.g. It's a watch.
   — ¿Es un reloj?
   — ¿Son relojes?

1) It's a white dog.
2) It's a long afternoon.
3) It's an old lighter.
4) It's a narrow street.
5) It's a thick book.
6) It's a small room.
7) It's a yellow raincoat.
8) It's a first lesson.
9) It's a big cat.
10) It's a green hat.

translate:

1) Can you repeat it, please?
2) The young child is bad.
3) That's not it.
4) The ashtray isn't green.
5) The streets aren't wide.
6) I'm sorry.
7) The broad's big and fat.
8) The guys are poor but interesting.
9) Time's up.
10) Darn it!
11) I apologize.
12) Good afternoon. How are you?
13) The books aren't thick.
14) The first lesson is long.
15) The girl's thin, me too.
16) The man isn't fat, me neither.
17) The lighter's old but good.
18) The kids are strong.
19) That correct. That's it.
20) The hat's little.
21) The first room is small.
22) The shoes are big.
23) The wall is red and blue.
24) The coat is black but the hat is navy blue.
25) Some books are interesting.
26) The rich girl is young.
27) The big telephone is red.
28) The yellow socks are small.

OPUESTOS (OPPOSITES) 1

learn by heart, and then ask someone to give you a test

1) **La chica es joven**   ≠   **vieja**
   The girl is young   old

2) **La mujer es gorda**   ≠   **delgada**
   The woman's fat   thin

3) **La mesa es pesada**   ≠   **liviana**
   The table's heavy   light

4) **La música está fuerte**   ≠   **suave**
   The music's loud   soft

5) **La calle es ancha**   ≠   **estrecha**
   The street's wide   narrow

6) **Miguel es rico**   ≠   **pobre**
   Mike's rich   poor

7) **El hombre es fuerte**   ≠   **débil**
   The man's strong   weak

8) **El papel es grueso**   ≠   **fino**
   The paper's thick   thin

9) **El cuarto es grande**   ≠   **pequeño**
   The room's big   small

10) **El hombre es bueno**   ≠   **malo**
    The man's good   bad

11) **El libro está sobre la mesa** ≠ **debajo de**
    The book is on the table   under

12) **Esta lección es la primera**   ≠ **la última**
    This lesson's first   last

VOCABULARIO

	traducción	sinónimo asociado	opuesto asociado
1. **también**	also ≠ neither	yo también = me too	yo tampoco = me neither
2. **¿que tal?**	how are you? ≠ fine, thank you, and you?	¿cómo estás? ¿cómo vas?, ¿cómo andas?	¿muy bien gracias, y tú?
3. **(el) hombre**	man ≠ woman	(el) tío, (el) chico, (el) tipo, (el) novio = boyfriend	(la) mujer, (la) chica = gal, (la) tía = broad, (la) novia = girlfriend
4. **(el) muchacho**	boy ≠ girl	(el) mozo, (el) chico, (el) chaval	(la) muchacha
5. **buenos días**	good morning	buenas tardes = good afternoon	buenas noches = good evening
6. **eso es**	that's right, that's it ≠ that's wrong	está bien, claro, ya, es correcto = that's correct, perfect	no es eso
7. **(el) niño**	child, kid	(el) crío, (el) nene = bebé = baby	(el) adulto
8. **(la) llave**	key		
9. **/(el) zapato/(el) calcetín**	/shoe/sock	botas = boots, zapatillas = slippers	
10. **¿puede repetirlo, por favor?**	could you repeat that, please?		
11. **/(el) cenicero /(la) cerilla /(el) mechero**	/ashtray/match /lighter	(el) fuego = light, (la) pipa = pipe	
12. **/verde/marrón**	/green/brown	amarillo = yellow, (el) color = colour	
13. **corto**	short ≠ long		largo
14. **/(el) sombrero /(el) abrigo**	/hat/coat	(el) impermeable = raincoat	
15. **lo siento**	I'm sorry	perdona = disculpa = dispensa = I apologize	
16. **es la hora**	time's up		
17. **(la) caja**	box	(el) cajón = drawer	

10

LECCIÓN 3

POSSESSIVE ADJECTIVES AND PRONOUNS

mi(s)	my	**el mío/la mía** **los míos/las mías**	mine
tu(s)	your	**el tuyo/la tuya** **los tuyos/las tuyas**	yours
su(s)	his, her, its, your, their	**el suyo/la suya** **los suyos/las suyas**	his, hers, its yours, theirs
nuestro(s) **nuestra(s)**	our	**el nuestro/la nuestra** **los nuestros/las nuestras**	ours
vuestro(s) **vuestra(s)**	your	**el vuestro/la vuestra** **los vuestros/las vuestras**	yours

note: This is less complicated than it seems. First you have to find out what
is owned (not who owns it) and follow the masculine or feminine,
singular or plural, of these words, e.g. nuestra madre = our mother,
nuestro padre = our father.
— tu, tus; vuestro, vuestros (an added difficulty!) are special words for
use by family, friends and lovers. For example; YOUR may be:
1) SU — formal
2) TU   tu coche = your car
   VUESTRO (of you both) casual   vuestro coche = your car

¿ES TU LIBRO? **SU**	Is it your book?
Sí, es mi libro.	Yes, it's my book.
Sí, es (el) mío.	Yes, it's mine.

note: After es/son the article is often dropped.

¿ES VUESTRO COCHE?	Is it your car?
	(of both of you)
Sí, es nuestro coche.	Yes, it's our car.
No, no es nuestro coche.	No, it's not our car.

note: **su** is more formal than **vuestro** which is for friends and . . . .

¿SON SUS LIBROS?	Are they his/her/your books?
Sí, son sus libros.	Yes, they're his/her/your books.
Sí, son suyos.	Yes, they're his/hers/yours.

¿DE QUIÉN ES EL LIBRO?	Whose book is it?
Es su libro (de él/ella/Vd.)	It's her/his/your book.
Es suyo.	It's his/hers/yours.

learn the numbers:

11 = **once**	16 = **dieciseis**
12 = **doce**	17 = **diecisiete**
13 = **trece**	18 = **dieciocho**
14 = **catorce**	19 = **diecinueve**
15 = **quince**	20 = **veinte**

translate:

1) Is it your scarf? No, it's hers.
2) Are they his boots? No, they're hers.
3) What's the matter?
4) Whose bag is it?
5) They aren't my turtlenecks, they're hers.
6) Thank you. You're welcome.
7) Are your slacks too short?
8) Get it?
9) They aren't your ties, they're his.
10) It doesn't matter.
11) What else? That's all.

translate in the negative form:

1) His gloves are small and nice.
2) My homework is easy.
3) Your new boots are big.
4) The last lesson is interesting.
5) Their clothes are small.
6) His beautiful new suit is black.
7) Our blackboard is wide.
8) My slacks are short.
9) Your turtleneck is light.
10) Her bag is old.
11) His tie is yellow.
12) Our lessons are happy.
13) Without a doubt, my jeans are big.
14) My table is heavy.
15) Your street is narrow.
16) Her car's small.
17) Their dresses are white and blue.

Insert the possessive pronouns:
e.g. Es mi suéter.
    — Es el mío.

1) Es su ropa. Es ... ...
2) Es mi camisa. Es ... ...
3) Son sus cigarrillos. Son ... ...
4) Es su corbata. Es ... ...
5) Es su traje nuevo. Es ... ...
6) Son vuestros guantes. Son ... ...
7) Es nuestra pizarra negra. Es ... ...
8) El mechero rojo es mi mechero. Es ... ...
9) El pantalón verde es su pantalón. Es ... ...
10) Es su vestido rojo. Es ... ...
11) Es nuestra última lección. Es ... ...
12) Es mi ropa vieja. Es ... ...
13) Es su pañuelo. Es ... ...
14) Son vuestros calcetines. Son ... ...
15) Son sus niños buenos. Son ... ...
16) Es su gran bolso. Es ... ...
17) Es tu pobre perro. Es ... ...
18) Es su primer hombre. Es ... ...
19) Es su tiza blanca. Es ... ...
20) Son sus botas negras. Son ... ...
21) Es su corbata azul. Es ... ...
22) Son vuestros nuevos libros. Son ... ...
23) Es su gran coche. Es ... ...
24) Son tus medias. Son ... ...
25) Son mis lecciones. Son ... ...
26) Son tus mesas. Son ... ...
27) Son tus perros. Son ... ...
28) Son nuestras mujeres. Son ... ...

VOCABULARIO

	traducción	sinónimo asociado	opuesto asociado
1. (el) vestido	dress	(la) falda = skirt, (la) blusa = blouse	
2. /(el) traje/(la) camisa/(la) corbata/(la) chaqueta	/suit/shirt/tie /jacket	(las) medias = stockings	
3. (el) pantalón	slacks	vaqueros = jeans	
4. /(el) bolso/(los) guantes/(el) bolsillo	/bag/gloves/pocket	(el) monedero = purse, (la) billetera = wallet	
5. ¿cómo se llama?	what's your name?	cuál es su nombre?	
6. me llamo . . .	my name is . . .		
6. (el) suéter	sweater	(el) jersey, (el) cuello vuelto = turtleneck	
8. (el) pañuelo	/scarf/handkerchief		
9. es cierto	certain, sure	seguro, sin duda = without a doubt	
10. muchas gracias	many thanks ≠ you're welcome	se lo agradezco	de nada, no hay de que
11. por favor	please	haga el favor	
12. vestidos	clothes	(la) ropa = clothing	
13. (la) pizarra	blackboard	(la) tiza = chalk	
14. mirar	to look at, watch	observar, contemplar	
15. ¿qué pasa?	what's the matter? what's wrong?	¿qué ocurre?, ¿qué tiene?	no pasa nada
16. no importa (nada)	it doesn't matter	es igual	
17. nada más	that's all ≠ what else?	es todo	¿qué más?
18. ¿entiende?	do you understand?	está claro?, comprende?, lo pesco = I get it	comprendo = I understand
19. explicar	to explain		

LECCIÓN 4

POSSESSION

El libro <u>de</u> Carmen.   Carmen's book.
Los libros <u>de</u> Carmen.   Carmen's books.

El coche <u>de los</u> hombres. The men's car.
      <u>de las</u> mujeres.   The women's car.

---

note: At last something easier in Spanish than in English! You say 'the book of Carmen' not 'Carmen's book'.

DE + EL → DEL   = OF THE

El libro del hombre.   The man's book.

---

note: No contraction for

    de la chica   of the girl
    de los ninos   of the children
    de las chicas   of the girls

Insert the correct form — de la, del, de los, de las:

1)	El libro . . . tío.	15)	La nariz . . . Juan.
2)	El vestido . . . chica.	16)	Los años . . . siglo.
3)	Los días . . . semana	17)	La ventana . . . cuarto.
4)	Los ojos . . . niños.	18)	Las orejas . . . perro.
5)	La boca . . . mujer.	19)	Las botas . . . chicos.
6)	El pie . . . hombre.	20)	La camisa . . . tío.
7)	Los meses . . . año.	21)	La lección . . . niños.
8)	La cabeza . . . niño.	22)	El coche . . . hombre.
9)	Las manos . . . chica.	23)	La lluvia . . . tarde.
10)	El brazo . . . niño.	24)	El bebé . . . muchacha.
11)	Los paraguas . . . chicas.	25)	Las horas . . . noche.
12)	Los dientes . . . niños.	26)	Las lecciones . . . libro.
13)	Los dedos . . . mano.	27)	La chaqueta . . . traje.
14)	los dedos . . . pie.		

¿QUÉ HORA ES?	What time is it?
Son las seis.	It's six o'clock.
Son las seis menos cuarto.	It's a quarter to six.
Son las seis y cuarto.	It's a quarter past six.
Son las seis y media.	It's six-thirty.

note: Es la una = It's one.

translate:

1) It's two-thirty.
2) It's a quarter to five.
3) It's ten to eight.
4) It's seven.
5) What time is it?

¿QUÉ?		=	WHAT? WHICH?	
	hombre(s)?		What	man/men?
¿Qué	**mujer(es)?**		(Which)	woman/women?
	coche(s)?			car/cars?

note: — ¿Cuál es . . . ? = What is . . . ?
— ¿Cuál? = Which one?

translate:

1) Peter's eyes are green.
2) How do you spell it?
3) The girl's mouth is large.
4) The woman who is tall is rich.
5) Wait a minute!
6) What's new? Nothing special.
7) Jane's face is thin.
8) The broad's legs are fat.
9) That's why he is poor.
10) The men's cars are big.
11) Which one is your car?
12) Why are the girls' sweaters long?
13) Which umbrella is yours?
14) Which man is yours?

17

VOCABULARIO

	traducción	sinónimo asociado	opuesto asociado
1. anda	go on ≠ wait	sigue, vamos	espera un momento
2. /la ventana /(la) puerta	/window/door	(el) escaparate = shop (US: store) window	
3. (el) paraguas	umbrella	(la) lluvia = rain	
4. (el) día	day	(la) semana = week	
5. /(el) año/(el) mes	/year/month	(el) siglo = century	
6. (el) domingo	Sunday, Monday, etc.	(el) lunes, (el) martes, (el) miércoles, (el) jueves, (el) viernes, (el) sábado	
7. /¿dónde? /¿cómo? /¿cuándo?	where?, how? when?	¿a dónde? = where to?, en = in, con = with	
8. aquí	here ≠ there		ahí = there, allí = over there
9. delante	in front of	en frente = across	detrás = behind
10. sobre	on ≠ under	encima de	debajo de
11. (la) cabeza	head	(la) cara	
12. cerca	near ≠ far from	junto a	lejos de
13. al lado de	next to	junto a	al otro lado = on the other side
14. /(el) ojo/(la) oreja/(la) nariz	/eye/ear/nose	ver = to see, oír = to hear	
15. /(la) mano/(el) brazo	/hand/arm	(el) dedo = finger	(el) pie = foot, (las) piernas = legs
16. /(la) boca/(la) lengua	/mouth/tongue	(el) diente = tooth	
17. ¿cómo se escribe?	how do you spell it?	¿cómo lo deletreas?	
18. ¿qué hay de nuevo?	what's new?	¿qué hay?	nada importante = nothing special
19. ¿por qué?	why?	por eso = that's why	porque = because
20. pero	but	sino (after negative clause)	

LECCIÓN 5

SER = TO BE			
yo soy	I am	**yo no soy**	I'm not
tú eres	you are	**tú no eres**	you aren't
él \} **es** **ella**	he she is it	**él** \} **no es** **ella**	he she isn't it
Vd. \}	you are	**Vd.** \}	you aren't
nosotros \} **somos** **nosotras**	we are	**nosotros** \} **no somos** **nosotras**	we aren't
vosotros \} **sois** **vosotras**	you are	**vosotros** \} **no sois** **vosotras**	you aren't
ellos \} **son** **ellas**	they are	**ellos** \} **no son** **ellas**	they aren't
Vds. \}	you are	**Vds.** \}	you aren't

rare

note: These subject pronouns are often left out in conversation:
  — abbreviated forms: usted = Vd., ustedes = Vds.
  — nosotros (masculine form) = we (men)
    nosotras (feminine form) = we (women)
  — REMEMBER 'tu' is for friends, family and lovers: the plural is
    'vosotros'

¿ES VD. AMERICANO?	Are you American?
Sí, soy americano.	Yes, I'm American.
No, no soy americano.	No, I'm not American.

note: use SER for permanent condition (blond, tall, man, American, job, etc.)
            time (it's six o'clock = son las seis)
            possession (it's mine = es mío)

ESTAR = TO BE

yo <u>estoy</u>	I am	**yo <u>no estoy</u>**	I'm not
tú <u>estás</u>	you are	**tú <u>no estás</u>**	you aren't
él ella } **<u>está</u>**	he she is it	**él ella** } **<u>no está</u>**	he she isn't it
Vd. }	you are	**Vd.** }	you aren't
nosotros nosotras } **<u>estamos</u>**	we are	**nosotros nosotras** } **<u>no estamos</u>**	we aren't
vosotros vosotras } **<u>estáis</u>**	you are	**vosotros vosotras** } **<u>no estáis</u>**	you aren't
ellos ellas } **<u>están</u>**	they are	**ellos ellas** } **<u>no están</u>**	they aren't
Vds. }	you are	**Vds.** }	you aren't

rare ← (handwritten note pointing to vosotros/vosotras rows)

¿ESTÁ ENFERMA?	Is she sick?
Sí, está enferma.	Yes, she is sick.
No, no está enferma.	No, she isn't sick.

note: use ESTAR for <u>health</u> (sick, well, etc.)
<u>location</u> (where is?)
<u>temporary condition</u> (cold, sad, on the table, etc.)

CAREFUL!!

¿ESTÁ AQUÍ DESDE HACE SEIS MESES?	Have you been here for six months?
Sí, estoy aquí desde hace seis meses.	Yes, I've been here for six months.
No, no estoy aquí desde hace seis meses.	No, I haven't been here for six months

note: the Spanish present is also used for our present perfect, i.e. for a past that continues!

20

PROBLEM!!

SER — ESTAR = TO BE

ES (ser)	ESTÁ (estar)
1) condition (what/who someone is: job, nationality, etc.)	1) location (where is?): ¿está en casa? = is she at home? ¿dónde está Madrid? = where is Madrid (located)? ¿dónde está? = where is she?
2) possession: es(el)mío = it's mine	2) health: ¿qué tal están? = how are they? estoy mal = I'm sick
3) permanent characteristics (colour, size, character, e.g. blue, big, bad): es malo = he's bad (US: mean)	3) temporary characteristics (sad, cold, tired, sick, on the table, on Monday): está triste = he's sad; estoy cansado = I'm tired
4) number: son diez dolares = it costs ten dollars	
5) time: son las tres = it's three o'clock.	

DON'T PANIC!! MISTAKES AREN'T CRUCIAL. IT WILL TAKE A LONG TIME TO DIFFERENTIATE.

translate:

1) She's bright.
2) He's a doctor.
3) Where are you?
4) The lessons aren't difficult.
5) I'm American.
6) The kids are mine.
7) You're pretty and rich.
8) He's a lawyer.
9) The boss is ugly.
10) The work's hard.
11) She's near me.
12) Are you Spanish?
13) Is this yours?
14) I'm tired.
15) The work's easy.
16) He's nice.
17) Why are you behind the door?
18) Who are they?
19) The teacher's mean.
20) It's ten o'clock.
21) The cat's on the table.
22) The book's under the chair.
23) You're in front of me.
24) Who is it?
25) It's mine.
26) I'm sick.
27) Where is he? He's here.
28) The man's tall.

```
ES = IT IS

es simpático        = it's nice       es verdad        = it's true
es interesante      = it's interesting es cierto        = it's sure
es aburrido         = it's boring      es fácil/difícil = it's easy/difficult
es bonito           = it's pretty      es posible       = it's possible
es temprano/tarde   = it's early/late  es preciso,      = it's necessary, a
es caro/barato      = it's expensive     necesario,       must
                      /cheap             menester
```

```
HACE = IT IS (tiempo = weather)

hace frío           = it's cold
hace calor          = it's hot
hace buen tiempo    = it's nice out
hace sol            = it's sunny
```

note: It's raining = llueve.
      It's snowing = nieva.

translate:

1) It's interesting.
2) It isn't possible.
3) Is it sunny?
4) It isn't cold.
5) Is it true?
6) It's too early.
7) Is it expensive?
8) No, it's cheap.
9) It's nice out.
10) It's boring.
11) It's hot.
12) It's pretty.
```
```

TAMBIÉN ≠ TAMPOCO	TOO, ALSO ≠ EITHER, NEITHER
Pilar es guapa y <u>yo también</u>.	Pilar is pretty and I am too.
Pilar no es guapa y <u>yo tampoco</u>.	Pilar isn't pretty and I'm not either.

translate and then put into the negative:

e.g. I'm Spanish and she is too.
- Soy española y ella también.
- No soy española, y ella tampoco.

1) My bike's fast and yours is too.
2) Her brother's crazy and so are you.
3) Your room's dirty and mine is too.
4) The cop's car's fast and mine is too.
5) His daughter's bright and yours is too.
6) Winter's cold and autumn (US: fall) is too.
7) Her bottle is empty and his is too.
8) Their teacher's boring and you are too.
9) Her guy's ugly and you are too.
10) I'm strong and so is she.
11) The clothing's clean and the room is too.
12) The cinema (US: movie) is crowded and the street is too.
13) We are here and they are too.
14) The cat's under the table and the dog is too.
15) Your hat is on the table and hers is too.
16) My jeans are dirty and yours are too.
17) Our turtlenecks are pretty and theirs are too.
18) Our kids are difficult and yours are too.
19) The soup's cold and I am too.
20) The boat's fast and the car is too.

OPUESTOS 2

1)	**La flor es <u>bonita</u>** The flower's pretty	≠	**fea** ugly
2)	**El abrigo está <u>sucio</u>** The coat's dirty	≠	**limpio** clean
3)	**El profesor tiene <u>razón</u>** The teacher's right	≠	**está confundido/se equivoca** wrong
4)	**La carretera es <u>peligrosa</u>** The road's dangerous	≠	**segura** safe
5)	**Las lecciones son <u>fáciles/sencillas</u>** The lessions are easy/simple	≠	**difíciles** hard/difficult
6)	**La regla es <u>larga</u>** The rule's long	≠	**corta** short
7)	**Mi bicícleta es <u>rápida</u>** My bike's fast	≠	**lenta** slow
8)	**La sopa está <u>fría</u>** The soup's cold	≠	**caliente** hot
9)	**La botella está <u>vacía</u>** The bottle's empty	≠	**llena** full
10)	**El caramelo está <u>azucarado</u>** The candy's sweet	≠	**agrio/amargo** sour/bitter
11)	**El techo es <u>alto</u>** The ceiling's high	≠	**bajo** low
12)	**Nuestro curso es <u>interesante</u>** Our lesson is interesting	≠	**aburrido/fastidioso** boring, dull
13)	**Mi hermano es <u>simpático</u>** My brother's nice	≠	**antipático** nasty (US mean)
14)	**El cine está <u>lleno</u>** The cinema's (US: movie's) crowded	≠	**vacío** empty
15)	**Esta chica es <u>inteligente</u>** This girl's bright	≠	**estúpida** stupid
16)	**Mi cuarto está <u>desordenado</u>** My room's sloppy	≠	**ordenado/arreglado** neat
17)	**empezar** to start, begin	≠	**acabar** to finish, stop
18)	**Mi piso es <u>caluroso</u>** My flat's hot	≠	**frío** cold

VOCABULARIO

	traducción	sinónimo asociado	opuesto asociado
1. a medio día	at noon ≠ midnight		media noche
2. por la mañana	in the morning ≠ at night	por la tarde = in the afternoon	por la noche = in the evening
3. /(el) verano/(la) primavera/(la) estación	summer, spring, season	(el) invierno = winter, (el) otoño = autumn (US: fall)	
4. ¿cuántos(as)?	how many?		
5. (la) clase	kind	(la) especie = sort = (el) tipo	
6. hoy	today	mañana = tomorrow	ayer = yesterday
7. ir	to go ≠ to come	irse = marcharse = to go away; salir = to go out; abandonar = to leave	venir, llegar, quedarse = to stay; volver = to come back
8. (la) hora	hour	media hora = half an hour	
9. (el) segundo	second	(el) minuto = minute	(el) rato = a while
10. enero	January	febrero, marzo, abril, mayo, junio, julio, agosto, septiembre, octubre, noviembre, diciembre	
11. /(el) coche/(el) avión/(el) barco /(el) tren/(el) taxi	car/plane/boat /train/taxi	(el) bote = boat, (el) carro = car, (el) autobús = bus, (el) metro = Underground (US subway), (la) estación = station	
12. preguntar	to ask a question ≠ to answer	hacer una pregunta, pedir = to ask	contestar, responder (la) contestación = answer
13. de acuerdo	all right, OK	ya, bueno, vale, entendido = it's a deal	no vale = no dice
14. ¡claro!	of course ≠ of course not	¡por supuesto!, ¡desde luego!, ¡absolutamente!, ¡por cierto!	¡claro que no!
15. loco	crazy, mad	chalado, chiflado	
16. tomar	to take ≠ leave	coger	dejar = to leave, to keep = guardar

LECCIÓN 6

AQUÍ = here	**AHÍ** = there	**ALLÁ** = over there
ESTE **ESTA** = this	**ÉSE** **ÉSA** = that	**AQUELLA** **AQUELLA** = that over there
ESTOS **ESTAS** = these	**ÉSOS** **ÉSAS** = those	**AQUELLOS** **AQUELLAS** = those over there

note: — Demonstrative adjectives agree in number and gender with the noun.
— An accent is added to the demonstrative adjective to form the demonstrative pronoun:

Quiero este libro y <u>ése</u> = I want this book and <u>that one</u>.

ESTO?	this?
¿QUÉ ES ESO?	What is that?
AQUELLO?	that (over there)?
Esto **Eso es un libro.** **Aquello**	This/that is a book.

note: Esto es bueno = This is good — this form is used when the 'this' is not identified (Está bueno = it's good).

learn the letters of the alphabet:

A-B-C-CH-D-E-F-G-H-I-J-L-LL-M-N-Ñ-O-P-Q-R-RR-S-T-U-V-X-Y-Z

HAY	=	THERE IS/THERE ARE

¿HAY UN HOMBRE AQUÍ? Is there a man here?

Sí, hay un hombre aquí. Yes, there's a man here.
No, no hay un hombre aquí. No, there isn't a man here.

¿HAY MUCHOS HOMBRES AQUÍ? Are there many men here?

Sí, hay muchos hombres aquí. Yes, there are many men here.
No, no hay muchos hombres aquí. No, there aren't many men here.

¿CUÁNTO(S)? = HOW MANY?

¿CUÁNTOS LIBROS HAY SOBRE LA MESA? How many books are there on the table?

Hay seis. There are six.

note: CUÁNTO(A/OS/AS) agrees in number and gender with the noun.

translate:

1) Are there thirty hours in a day?
2) Are these roads dangerous? Which ones are?
3) Are there taxis in the streets this afternoon?
4) Are there crazy men in this room?
5) Are there empty bottles on the table?
6) Is there candy on the table?
7) Are there boring teachers in the room?
8) There are three pretty cars in front of my window. Which ones?
9) There is a full bottle under the table.
10) There is a boring lesson in the book. Which one?

learn the numbers:

20 = **veinte**	70 = **setenta**
30 = **treinta**	80 = **ochenta**
40 = **cuarenta**	90 = **noventa**
50 = **cincuenta**	100 = **cien(to)**
60 = **sesenta**	1000 = **mil**

note: 21 = **veintiuno**, etc., but **treinta y uno, cuarenta y dos**, etc.

27

translate:

1) Estos bolsos están sobre la mesa.
2) Esos trajes son pequeños para estos hombres.
3) Estos relojes son nuestros y ésos son suyos.
4) Ese abrigo es mío, y éste es tuyo.
5) Esos tíos están lejos de Carmen, pero su novio está cerca.
6) Esas calles son largas pero ésta es estrecha.
7) Estas botellas están vacías pero esas botellas están llenas.
8) Esa mujer es americana pero estas mujeres son españolas.
9) Este médico es el mío, y ése es el tuyo.
10) Esta casa es nuestra y aquélla también.
11) Estos coches y aquéllos son bonitos.
12) Esto es bueno.
13) Este trabajo es muy aburrido.
14) Ese tío es loco y aquéllos también.

translate:

1) That broad is crazy but interesting.
2) Is that guy boring? This one isn't.
3) That car's big, but these aren't.
4) Which kid is yours? This one.
5) Is that house over there yours?
6) No, but this one is.
7) These doctors are Spanish and those are American.
8) These books are Carmen's and those over there are mine.
9) That coat over there is mine and this one is also.
10) Those kids are pretty and this one is too.
11) This shoe here and that one over there is mine.
12) Are these chairs yours? No, but this one is.
13) Those teachers are nice and these are too.
14) The lawyer over there is mine. Is this one yours?

ADVERBIOS Y FRASES (ADVERBS AND PHRASES) 1

1. a causa de	because of	14. — muy	— very
2. pocas veces	rarely	— bastante	— enough
3. a menudo	often	15. — al menos	at least
4. casi	almost, nearly	— por lo menos	
5. — de todos modos — de todas maneras — de todas formas	at any rate, in any case	16. hace	ago
		17. — a lo más	— at the most
		— a lo menos	— at the least
		18. — claro está	naturally
		— por supuesto	
		19. no . . . más	not . . . any more
6. — apenas — poco	scarcely, hardly	20. sin	without
7. hasta	until, till	21. excepto	except
8. — general- mente — de costum- bre — por lo común	usually	22. — los dos — ambos	both
		23. junto(s)	together
		24. — ¿dónde? ¿en dónde?	— where?
		— ¿de dónde?	— where from?
9. el día que	the day when	— ¿por dónde?	— which way?
10. — nunca — jamás	never, ever	— ¿a dónde?	— where to?
		25. — una vez	— once
11. siempre	always	— una vez por semana	— once a week
12. en punto	on the dot (time)	— una vez más	— once more
		— otra vez	— again
13. — mucho — un poco	— a lot, much — a little, a bit	26. a la vez	at the same time

VOCABULARIO

	traducción	sinónimo asociado	opuesto asociado
1. me gustaría presentarle	I'd like you to meet ≠ pleased to meet you	me gustaría que conociera . . .	encantado(a); encontrar = to meet (bump into)
2. /¿quién?/¿qué?	/who?/which?	¿cuál? = which one?	
3. /(el) médico /(el) abogado	/doctor/lawyer	hospital = hospital, enfermera = nurse	
4. /(el) estudiante /(la) escuela	/student/school	(el) alumno = pupil, (el) colegio	(el) profesor = teacher = (el) maestro
5. /(el) hombre de negocios/los negocios	/businessman/business	un negociante	
6. la poli	cop	(la) policía, (el) gris, (el) verde	
7. /(el) jefe/(la) oficina	/boss, chief/office	director = director, (el) despacho	(el) empleado = employee
8. demasiado	too (much) ≠ not enough	suficiente	insuficiente; bastante = enough
9. (el) problema	problem	dificultad	
10. (el) trabajo	work, job	(la) tarea	descanso = rest
11. me parece que sí	I think so	creo/pienso que sí, supongo = I suppose ya lo creo = of course	¿le parece? do you think so?
12. ya uno ya otro	either (one) ≠ neither one	o uno u otro (otro (a) = other)	ni uno ni otro
13. ¡qué lástima!	what a pity! ≠ thank heavens!	¡qué pena!	¡gracias a Dios!
14. ¿qué significa?	what does it mean?	¿qué quiere decir?, el significado = meaning	es decir = I mean
15. (el) cine	cinema (US: movies)	(la) película = film	
16. (la) secretaria	secretary	(la) mecanógrafa = typist	
17. sobre todo	above all	por encima de todo, en especial	

LECCIÓN 7

There are three groups of verbs in Spanish: <u>AR</u>, <u>ER</u>, <u>IR</u>.

TIEMPO PRESENTE (present tense) — VERBS IN <u>AR</u>

HABLAR = to speak

habl<u>o</u>	I speak
habl<u>as</u>	you speak
habl<u>a</u>	he speaks
	she speaks
	you speak
se habl<u>a</u>	one speaks
habl<u>amos</u>	we speak
habl<u>áis</u>	you speak
habl<u>an</u>	they speak

---

note: — The above endings are added to the stem of the verb.
— The use of 'se' is extremely common, and can be translated by: you, he, she, they.
— 'yo', 'tu', etc. are often dropped — hablo = I speak — except in the case of Vd.
— the Spanish present is for:
1) an action in the midst of being done: habla = he's <u>speaking</u>.
2) a repeated action: habla a menudo = he <u>often speaks</u>.
3) an action started in the past that still goes on (the English present perfect): hace una hora que hable = he's <u>been speaking</u> for an hour.

HABLA VD. A MENUDO INGLÉS?

Do you often speak English?

Sí, hablo a menudo inglés. — Yes, I often speak English.
No, no hablo a menudo inglés. — No, I don't often speak English.

```
¿QUIÉN? = WHO? WHOM?          ¿QUÉ? = WHAT?
¿Quién habla?  Who's speaking?   ¿Qué comes?  What are you eating?
```

```
A + EL → AL
Llego al mediodía.              I'm coming at noon.
Voy al cine.                    I'm going to the movies.
```

note: No contraction is used for a la:
    a la chica → a los/las . . . .

```
PERSONAL A
Conozco a Juan.                 I know John.
Hablo a Carmen.                 I am speaking to Carmen.
```

note: — 'a' is placed after the verb when it is followed by a person's name
      (when the direct object is a person).

```
¿HABLA DESDE HACE UNA           Has she been speaking for an hour?
HORA?
Sí, habla desde hace una hora.  Yes, she's been speaking for an hour.
No, no habla desde hace una hora.  No, she hasn't been speaking for an
                                hour.
```

note: This special use of the present for the English 'past which continues' is
very, very often used.

translate:

1) Conozco a Carmen desde hace dos años.
2) Siempre quiere lo mismo.
3) Quizás podemos ir ahora.
4) Vuelve a menudo muy tarde.
5) Suelo comer mucho.
6) Esta cosa vale por lo menos dos dólares.
7) Llueve sobre todo en otoño.
8) ¿Puede Vd. traerle un café a Pedro?
9) Estamos aquí desde hace cinco años.
10) La poli suele ser dura.
11) ¿Podemos hacer este trabajo?
12) Lee este libro desde hace una semana.
13) Tengo mucha prisa para comprar aquel coche.
14) Todos los días tomo la siesta por la tarde.

translate:

1) Do you usually understand the teacher?
2) I suppose you know the answer.
3) Am I right?
4) It's sunny today.
5) He's been a doctor for two years.
6) Do you know the teacher well?
7) Whose is it? It's hers.
8) Can you come this evening?
9) Does this thing belong to you?
10) He isn't a doctor, he isn't a lawyer either.
11) Do you want to go with that crazy guy?
12) No, I want to take a walk with Paul.
13) Have you known Carmen since the summer?
14) I'm not used to coming on time.

```
SPECIAL NEGATIVES
NO . . . MÁS        No habla más.              He doesn't speak any
                                               more.
NO . . . NUNCA      No habla nunca.            He never speaks.
NO . . . MÁS QUE    No habla más que francés.⎫ He only speaks French.
NO . . . SINO       No habla sino francés.    ⎬
NO . . . TODAVÍA    No esta aquí todavía.     ⎭ He isn't here yet.
NO . . . NADA       No dice nada.              He doesn't say anything.
NO . . . NADIE      No habla con nadie.        He isn't speaking to
                                               anyone.
```

note: — Get used to these special negatives, they are very often used!!
  — YA NO = no more.

translate:

1) No quiero beber más que una cerveza.
2) El jefe no tiene más que un coche.
3) No como con nadie.
4) No vuelve nunca tarde.
5) No puedo hacer este trabajo todavía.
6) No quiero nada.
7) Este hombre no bebe más que vino.
8) No tiene razón nunca.

translate:

1) Are you used to drinking a lot?
2) I don't see anyone.
3) Her guy never eats at home.
4) We want only one.
5) It isn't nice out yet.
6) I'm only reading one book this month.
7) You can't do anything.
8) It never rains in summer in Madrid.

translate:

1) Siempre fumo después de comer.
2) Los niños nunca juegan en clase.
3) Trabaja generalmente por la tarde hasta las seis.
4) Nunca recuerdas mi nombre.
5) Sueño por lo menos cada noche.
6) Piensa que hace frío.
7) ¿Por qué habláis desde hace una hora?
8) ¿Encuentras a menudo hombres interesantes?
9) Estudiamos pocas veces los sábados.
10) Estoy aquí desde hace un año.
11) Me da clase de inglés todos los días.
12) Siempre haces demasiadas preguntas.
13) Nunca deja a los niños solos.
14) A menudo contesto rápidamente.

translate:

1) We've been playing for an hour.
2) How much do the books cost?
3) What do you think of it?
4) She's been talking for two hours.
5) I'm at last beginning this work.
6) Both start working at six in the morning.
7) Who's speaking?
8) Are you speaking to your boss?
9) We're stopping work now.
10) I've been studying Spanish for a year.
11) I'm talking to the children.
12) We've been here for five years.
13) It scarcely snows in Madrid.
14) We usually wear coats and boots in winter.

VERBOS IRREGULARES DE PRIMER GRUPO: AR (presente)

DAR = to give
doy
damos
dan

EMPEZAR = to begin
empiezo
empezamos
empiezan

PENSAR = to think
pienso
pensamos
piensan

ACORDAR = to agree
acuerdo
acordamos
acuerdan

RECORDAR = to
remember
recuerdo
recordamos
recuerdan

ACOSTAR(SE) to go
to bed.
(me) acuesto
(nos) acostamos
(se) acuestan

ESTAR = to be
estoy
estamos
están

SENTAR(SE) = to sit
(me) siento
(nos) sentamos
(se) sientan

DESPERTAR = to
wake up
despierto
despertamos
despiertan

JUGAR = to play
juego
jugamos
juegan

COMENZAR = to start
comienza
comenzamos
comienzan

SOÑAR = to dream
sueño
soñamos
sueñan

COSTAR = to cost
cuesto
costamos
cuestan

CERRAR = to shut
cierro
cerramos
cierran

CONTAR = to count
cuento
contamos
cuentan

ROGAR = to be
ruego
rogamos
ruegan

ENCONTRAR = to meet
encuentro
encontramos
encuentran

VOCABULARIO

	traducción	sinónimo asociado	opuesto asociado
1. ¿y Vd. que?	what about you?		
2. /llover/(la) lluvia	/to rain/rain	llover a cántaros = to pour	
3. nevar	to snow	(la) nieve = snow, (el) tiempo = weather	
4. una vez	once, one time	dos veces = twice	nunca = never; siempre = always; a menudo = often
5. /estudiar/ escribir	/to study/to write	aprender = to learn	to teach = enseñar
6. /(el) sol/(la) luna	/sun/moon	hace sol = it's sunny	(la) sombra = shade, (la) nube = cloud
7. mucho	much ≠ a little, a bit	un montón de, la mayoría de = most of; la mayor parte de	un poco, poquito, poquitín, muy poco; solo = único = solamente = only
8. /(la) tormenta /(el) viento	/storm/wind	(el) trueno = thunder	hace buen tiempo = it's nice out
9. vestirse	to get dressed	llevar = to wear	desvestirse = to get undressed
10. dormirse	to go to sleep ≠ to wake up	irse a la cama = to go to bed; (la) siesta = nap	despertarse = to wake up; levantarse = to get up
11. (la) cosa	thing	(el) chisme = cacharro = stuff; (el) artículo = item	
12. tengo prisa	I'm in a hurry ≠ I have the time	correr = to run	no tengo tiempo = I don't have the time
13. fumar	to smoke	(el) cigarro = cigarrette; (el) puro = cigar	
14. /lavarse /arreglarse	/to get washed /to get ready	prepararse	
15. ir de compras	to go shopping	ir de tiendas	
16. /en el colegio/en el trabajo/en casa /en el hotel	/at school/at work /at home/at the hotel	at 8. p.m. = a las ocho de la tarde	

LECCIÓN 8

TIEMPO PRESENTE — VERBS IN <u>ER</u>

APRENDER = to learn

aprend<u>o</u>	I learn
aprend<u>es</u>	you learn
aprend<u>e</u>	she he learns
	you learn
se aprend<u>e</u>	one learns
aprend<u>emos</u>	we learn
aprend<u>eis</u>	you learn
aprend<u>en</u>	they you learn

¿APRENDE VD. LA LENGUA ESPAÑOLA DESDE HACE UN AÑO?	Have you been learning Spanish for a year?
Sí, aprendo la lengua española desde hace un año.	Yes, I have been learning Spanish for a year.
No, no aprendo la lengua española desde hace un año.	No, I haven't been learning Spanish for a year.

¿COME VD. TEMPRANO TODOS LOS DIAS?	Do you eat early every day?
Sí, como temprano todos los días.	Yes, I eat early every day.
No, no como temprano todos los días.	No, I don't eat early every day.

note: Remember the Spanish present is also for a past action which still goes on: Hace una hora que comen = They've been eating for an hour.

note: These special negatives are rather tricky but extremely important in the spoken language and can be used with any verbs.

translate:

1) Nunca tenemos bastante tiempo.
2) No tiene más que dos hijos.
3) No hay nadie en el cuarto.
4) No están aquí todavía.
5) No habla más que español.
6) No da nada a su mujer.
7) No hablo con nadie.

translate:

1) I'm not thinking about anything.
2) He is never with you.
3) I have only one child. (two ways)
4) He isn't here yet.
5) She never meets anyone on holiday/vacation.
6) She only plays with the children at night. (two ways)
7) I have nothing.

VERBOS IRREGULARES DE SEGUNDO GRUPO: ER (presente)

VALER = to be worth	**VER** = to see	**QUERER** = to want
valgo	veo	quiero
valemos	vemos	queremos
valen	ven	quieren

HACER = to make	**TRAER** = to bring	**CAER** = to fall
hago	traigo	caigo
hacemos	traemos	caemos
hacen	traen	caen

SABER = to know
sé
sabemos
saben

PODER = can
puedo
podemos
pueden

HABER = to have
he
hemos
han

VOLVER = to become
vuelvo
volvemos
vuelven

ENTENDER = to understand
entiendo
entendemos
entienden

PARECER = to seem
parezco
parecemos
parecen

PARECERSE = to resemble

ESTABLECER = to set up
establezco
establecemos
establecen

LEER = to read
leo
leemos
leen

DOLER = to hurt
duele
dolemos
duelen

PERDER = to lose
pierdo
perdemos
pierden

PONER = to put
pongo
ponemos
ponen

PONERSE = to put on

SER = to be
soy
somos
son

CABER = to contain
quepo
cabemos
caben

OLER = to smell
huelo
olemos
huelen

CONOCER = to know
conozco
conocemos
conocen

PERTENECER = to belong
pertenezco
pertenecemos
pertenecen

NACER = to be born
nazco
nacemos
nacen

LLOVER = to rain
llueve

AGRADECER = to thank
agradezco
agradecemos
agradecen

PROPONER = to suggest
propongo
proponemos
proponen

TENER = to have
tengo
tenemos
tienen

SOLER = to be used to
suelo
solemos
suelen

MOVER = to move
muevo
movemos
mueven

RECONOCER = to recognise
reconozco
reconocemos
reconocen

CONVENCER = to convince
convenzo
convencemos
convencen

PROTEGER = to protect
protejo
protegemos
protegen

COGER = to take
cojo
cogemos
cogen

MERECER = to deserve
merezco
merecemos
merecen

VOCABULARIO

	traducción	sinónimo asociado	opuesto asociado
1. cada (día)	every (day), each	todo los días	todos (as) = all
2. /en los Estados Unidos/en mi oficina/en mi cuarto	/in the USA/in my office/in my room	in an hour = dentro de una hora	
3. quizá(s)	perhaps, maybe	tal vez, puede ser	
4. /no ... más/no ... más que	/not ... any more /only	/ya no = no more /solamente, solo	todavía = still
5. /querer/querer a	/to want/to love	desear = to wish	
6. gustar	to like (me gustan = I like ...) ≠ to hate	adorar = to adore, estar loco por = to be crazy about	odiar = no le puedo ver = soportarle = I can't stand him
7. enseñar	to show, to teach	indicar, mostrar	
8. escuchar	to listen to		oír = to hear
9. esperar	to wait for, to hope	espero = ojalá = I hope	
10. trabajar	to work		descansar = to rest
11. es temprano	it's early ≠ late		es tarde
12. feliz	happy ≠ sad	alegre, contento	triste
13. llego tarde	I'm late ≠ early	a tiempo = on time	llego temprano = por adelantado
14. interesante	interesting ≠ boring	apasionante	aburrido, una lata = a drag, fastidioso
15. ¿de quién es?	whose is it?	¿a quién le toca? = whose turn is it?	
16. andar	/to walk/to work	pasearse, dar un paseo = to go for a walk/marchar	no marcha = no anda it doesn't work
17. esto	this ≠ that		eso
18. antes (de)	before ≠ after		trás, después (de)

LECCIÓN 9

TENER = TO HAVE

tengo	I have
tienes	you have
tiene	he/she/has
	you have
tenemos	we have
teneis	you have
tienen	they have

---

note: HABER also means 'to have', but is only an auxiliary verb.

¿TIENE DINERO?	Do you (does she/he) have some money?
Sí, tengo dinero.	Yes, I have some money.
No, no tengo dinero.	No, I haven't any money.

ALGUNOS/UNOS = SOME

¿Tiene Vd. $\frac{\text{algunas}}{\text{unas}}$ cerillas?	Have you <u>some</u> matches?
Sí, tengo $\frac{\text{unas}}{\text{algunas}}$ cerillas.	Yes, I have <u>some</u> matches.
Sí, tengo <u>algunas</u>.	Yes, I have <u>some</u>.
No, no tengo <u>ninguna</u> cerilla.	No, I <u>don't</u> have <u>any</u> matches.
No, no tengo <u>ninguna</u>.	No, I <u>don't</u> have <u>any</u>.

¿CUÁNTO(A,OS,AS)?	=	HOW MANY?
¿Cuántos tiene?		How many have you?
Tengo diez.		I have ten.

TENER	=	TO BE
tener hambre		to be hungry
tener sed		to be thirsty
tener . . . años		to be . . . years old
tener sueño		to be sleepy
tener frío		to be cold
tener calor		to be hot
tener miedo		to be afraid
tener razón		to be right
tener éxito		to be successful
tener costumbre		to be used to
tener suerte		to be lucky
tener cuidado		to be careful
tener prisa		to be in a hurry

translate:

1) The teacher isn't always right.
2) Have you some time this afternoon?
3) How many cigarettes have you?
4) That businessman is always successful.
5) I'm not hungry but I'm thirsty.
6) Have you some sandwiches. Yes, we have some.
7) In any case, I'm afraid.
8) You're almost right.
9) We never have money.
10) She only has two dollars. Have you any?
11) I'm not lucky any more.
12) Together they're fifteen years old.
13) I'm often cold in the winter and hot in the summer.
14) She's rarely sleepy.
15) The boss's secretary is never wrong.
16) We're used to drinking a lot of beer once a week.
17) She always drinks beer at the restaurant.
18) We're in a hurry, but on the other hand, I want a good meal.

TO HAVE TO — how to translate

Tengo que)
Hay que
Debo   I must)
                    ir   ) go
Es preciso   I have to)
    menester
    necesario /

note: All these are used interchangeably to express 'have to'; the infinitives of the verbs used are — tener, haber, deber.

¿TIENE QUE IR AHORA?   Do you have to go now?

Sí, tengo que ir ahora.   Yes, I have to go now.
No, no tengo que ir ahora.   No, I don't have to go now.

---

translate:

1) We have to eat quickly.
2) You don't have to speak with her alone.
3) You must come on time every day.
4) You have to learn quickly.
5) It's necessary to eat to live.
6) You must rest from time to time.
7) I have to go now.
8) You don't have to tell me if you don't want to.

translate:

1) Tenemos siempre que esperar a Carmen.
2) Tenemos que comer en vez de hablar.
3) No debes llegar tarde.
4) Tengo que ir ahora.
5) Es necesario trabajar en la vida.
6) ¿Debe volver ahora?
7) Tengo que decirle algo a Vd.
8) Tenemos que salir más tarde.

ADVERBIOS Y FRASES 2

1. **solo**	alone	13. **exactamente**	exactly
2. **approximada-** **mente**	about, around	14. — **para, por**	— to
3. **entre**	between	— **a fin de que**	— in order to, so that
4. — **al final**	at last	— **para que, de** **modo**	
— **por fin**		— **de modo** **que**	— in order that
— **finalmente**		— **de manera** **que**	
5. **mientras**	in the meantime		
6. — **quizás**	perhaps, maybe	15. **a punto de**	about to
— **tal vez**		16. **incluso antes**	even before
— **acaso**		17. — **súbitamente**	all of a sudden, suddenly
7. **a pesar de**	in spite of	— **de repente**	
8. — **en lugar de**	instead of	18. **en cambio**	on the other hand
— **en vez de**		19. **inmediata-** **mente**	immediately
9. — **de vez en** **cuando**	— from time to time	20. **sino**	if not
— **a veces**	— now and then	21. **hacia**	towards
— **algunas** **veces**	— sometimes	22. **al principio**	at first
10. — **así**	thus, therefore so, then	23. — **todavía no**	— not yet
— **pues**		— **ya**	— already
— **entonces**		24. **al fin y al** **cabo**	all in all, when all's said and done
11. **sin embargo**	however	25. **lo antes** **posible**	as soon as possible
12. **aunque**	even, although	26. **de alguna** **manera**	in some way
		27. **siempre que**	whenever

VOCABULARIO

	traducción	sinónimo asociado	opuesto asociado
1. caro	expensive	que tiene valor, que vale mucho	barato = cheap
2. hablar con	to speak to	charlar = to chat	
3. /a pie/en metro /de vacaciones	/on foot/on the underground (US: subway)/on vacation		
4. ahora	now, at present	en este momento, de momento, ahora mismo = right now = en seguida	pronto = soon, más tarde = later, ya no = not now
5. para	for, to	por	
6. (la) comida	meal	(el) bocadillo = sandwich	
7. /(el) desayuno /(el) almuerzo /(la) cena	/breakfast/lunch /supper	la hora de comer = lunchtime, desayunar = to have breakfast, cenar = to dine	
8. probar	to taste	sírvete = help yourself	
9. /(el) cuchillo /(el) tenedor/(la) cuchara/(la) servilleta	/knife/fork/spoon /napkin	cucharita = coffee spoon	
10. tengo que	I have to, must	debo, hay que	
11. decir	to say	contar = to tell	
12. (el) restaurante	restaurant	(el) menú = menu	
13. /ordenar/(el) camarero	/to order/waiter	(la) camarera = waitress	
14. /(la) taza/(el) vaso/(el) agua/ agua potable	/cup/glass/water drinking water	agua del grifo = tap water, (el) platillo = saucer, (la) botella = bottle	
15. /(el) pan/(la) mantequilla	/bread/butter	pan tostado = toast	
16. (la) carne	meat	(el) filete = steak	
17. (el) plato	plate	(la) fuente = dish	
18. /comer/beber	/eat/drink	(la) bebida = drink	

LECCIÓN 10

TIEMPO PRESENTE — VERBS IN <u>IR</u>

VIVIR = to live

vi**vo**	I live
vi**ves**	you live
vi**ve**	he lives she you live
viv**imos**	we live
viv**ís**	you live
viv**en**	they live

note: The endings for this group are the same as for the ER group, except for 'nosotros' and 'vosotros'

¿VIVE EN MADRID?   Do you (does she) live in Madrid?

Sí, vivo en Madrid.   Yes, I live in Madrid.
No, no vivo en Madrid.   No, I don't live in Madrid.

¿VIVE AQUÍ DESDE HACE MUCHO?
DESDE HACE CINCO AÑOS?

Have you been living here for a long time?
five years?

Sí, vivo aquí desde hace mucho.
5 años.

Yes, I've been living here for a long time.
five years.

No, no vivo aquí desde hace mucho.
5 años.

No, I've not been living here for a long time.
five years.

---

note: Remember the use of the Spanish present for a past which continues.

No habla más.	I don't speak any more.
No oigo nada.	I don't hear anything.
No vivo más que aquí. ⎱	I only live here.
No vivo sino aquí. ⎰	
No vivo nunca aquí.	I never live here.
No veo a nadie.	I don't see anyone.
No me duermo todavía.	I'm not sleeping yet.

note: I don't live here any more = Ya no vivo aquí.

translate:

1) Duermo por la tarde de vez en cuando.
2) Al fin y al cabo sale a menudo.
3) No viene nunca.
4) No digo nada a nadie.
5) Pido un café solo en vez de un café con leche.
6) No lo siento más.
7) Prefiero vino. ¿Y usted?
8) No quiero más a Pablo, pero todavía viene todos los días.
9) Escribo la carta, aunque no tengo mucho tiempo.
10) La profesora no repite nunca la lección.
11) No hablan más de Madrid.
12) Ahora, viven en Nueva York, desde hace dos años.
13) Los alumnos repiten todavía la lección.
14) Los niños no se duermen todavía.
15) Antes de salir tenemos que pagar la cuenta.
16) Todos morimos un día.
17) Esta hora conviene al profesor.
18) Seguimos trabajando a pesar de la lluvia.

VERBOS IRREGULARES DE TERCER GRUPO: IR (presente)

OÍR = to hear
oigo
oimos
oyen

DECIR = to say
digo
decimos
dicen

VENIR = to come
vengo
venimos
vienen

PREVENIR = to warn
prevengo
prevenimos
previenen

CONVENIR = to suit
convengo
convenimos
convienen

SALIR = to go
salgo
salimos
salen

DORMIR = to sleep
duermo
dormimos
duermen

MORIR = to die
muero
morimos
mueren

SENTIR = to feel
siento
sentimos
sienten

PREFERIR = to prefer
prefiero
preferimos
prefieren

DIVERTIR(SE) = to enjoy
(me) divierto
(nos) divertimos
(se) divierten

REPETIR = to repeat
repito
repetimos
repiten

SEGUIR = to follow
sigo
seguimos
siguen

PEDIR = to ask
pido
pedimos
piden

CONSEGUIR = to reach
consigo
conseguimos
consiguen

VESTIR(SE) = to get dressed
(me) visto
(nos) vestimos
(se) visten

REÑIR = to quarrel
riño
reñimos
riñen

CONCLUIR = to conclude
concluyo
concluimos
concluyen

HUIR = to escape
huyo
huimos
huyen

CONSTRUIR = to build
construyo
construimos
construyen

CONDUCIR = to drive
conduzco
conducimos
conducen

DISTINGUIR = to distinguish
distingo
distinguimos
distinguen

ELEGIR = to choose
elijo
elegimos
elijen

REIR = to laugh
río
reímos
ríen

DESVESTIR(SE) = to undress
(me) desvisto
(nos) desvestimos
(se) desvisten

SERVIR = to serve
servo
servimos
se
sirven

DESPEDIR(SE) = to leave off
(me) despido
(nos) despedimos
(se) despiden

SONREIR = to smile
sonrío
sonreímos
sonríen

49

VOCABULARIO

	traducción	sinónimo asociado	opuesto asociado
1. no puedo más	I'm full ≠ hungry	tengo bastante	tengo hambre
2. (la) sal	salt ≠ pepper	(la) especia = spices	(la) pimienta
3. /(el) pollo/(la) ternera	/chicken/veal	puerco, cerdo = pork	
4. poco hecha	rare ≠ well done	vuelta y vuelta = very rare	bien hecha, a punto = medium
5. /(el) cordero /(el) pescado	/lamb/fish		
6. (la) patata	potato	patatas fritas = French fries; (el) arroz = rice	
7. /(la) sopa/(los) entremeses	/soup/hors d'œuvres		
8. /(el) tomate /(la) lechuga	/tomato/lettuce	(la) ensalada	
9. /¿cuánto es?/(el) precio	/how much is it? /price	¿cuánto vale?, ¿qué precio?, ¿cuánto cuesta?	gratis = de balde = free
10. /(el) pastel /(el) postre	/cake/dessert	(el) helado = ice-ice-cream	
11. /(la) cuenta /(la) propina	/bill/tip	servicio incluído = tip included	
12. /(el) té/(el) café	/tea/coffee	(la) leche = milk; (el) azúcar = sugar; café solo = black coffee	
13. /(el) huevo/(el) jamón/(el) vino (el) queso	/egg/ham/wine	(la) cerveza = beer (el) tocino = bacon	
14. /(la) verdura /(el) guisante	/vegetables/pea	(la) legumbre, zanahoria = carrot, judía verde = runner (US: string) beans	
15. ¿qué te gustaría?	what would you care for?	¿de qué tienes ganas? = ¿qué te apetece?	quisiera = I would like
16. me gusta	I like, enjoy	me encanta, me apetece, me alegro	no me gusta

LECCIÓN 11

DIRECT OBJECT PRONOUNS

These answer the question:

¿QUIÉN? = WHO(M)?

subject		*object*	
yo	I	**me**	me
tu	you	**te**	you
el	he, it	**le, lo**	him, it
ella	she	**la**	her
Vd.	you	**le**	you
nosotros(as)	we	**nos**	us
vosotros(as)	you	**os**	you
ellos	they (masc.)	**les, los**	them
ellas	they (fem.)	**las**	them
Vds.	you	**les**	you

note: — 'os' is rare in South America: use los/las instead.
       — 'lo' = it.

¿ME VE VD.?	Do you see me?
Sí, le veo	Yes, I see you.
No, no le veo.	No, I don't see you.

```
POSITIVE

I see me.                    Me veo.
I see you.                   Te/le/les veo.
I see him/it.                Le/lo veo.
I see her.                   La veo.
I see us.                    Nos veo.
I see them.                  Los/las veo.
```

```
NEGATIVE

No me veo.                   I don't see me.
No te veo.                   I don't see you.
No le veo.                   I don't see him.
No la veo.                   I don't see her.
No lo veo.                   I don't see it.
No nos veo.                  I don't see us.
No os veo.                   I don't see you.
No las/los veo.              I don't see them.
```

```
                — te veo (friend)
                — le veo (formal singular)
I see you
                — os veo (friends plural)
                — les veo (formal plural)
```

note: CAREFUL of these four ways of translating 'you'!

insert the correct pronoun instead of the noun:

e.g. Veo este perro.

    — Lo veo.

1) No entiendo esta lección.
2) No viven en esta casa.
3) No conozco muy bien a estas personas.
4) No vemos a menudo las películas de este tío.
5) No quieren este postre.
6) ¿Entiende al profesor?
7) No conoce a esta mujer.
8) Podemos comprar este viejo sillón.
9) Como queso cada día.
10) Tengo que ir a comprar legumbres para la cena.
11) Puedo ver a mi profesor durante una hora.
12) A menudo espera a Pedro y a mí después de la clase.
13) Quiero estos pasteles.
14) Veo poco a vuestro hermano.
15) De vez en cuando toma mi abrigo.
16) Empezamos la clase por un test.
17) Aprendemos los verbos.
18) Compra el coche la semana próxima.
19) Tomamos el avión a las ocho de la tarde.
20) Abren la puerta cada diez minutos.
21) Hace bien el trabajo.
22) No reconozco a la mujer.
23) Pone los libros sobre la mesa.
24) ¿Conoce la respuesta?
25) Leen los nuevos libros.
26) Bebemos el café cuando es bueno.
27) Veo a esta persona en mi oficina.
28) El profesor no comprende a los alumnos.

```
CAREFUL!!

Van a verle.                        They are going to see him.
Quieren escucharlos.                They want to listen to them.
```

note: When the pronoun is the object of an infinitive, it follows and is attached to the verb.

translate:

1) I don't like this hard cake and I don't want it.
2) I can't see them with the boss.
3) We can't hear you.
4) I'm not sending it to you.
5) The teacher is boring and we don't often listen to him.
6) For how long haven't you see her?
7) You have to go upstairs to find it.
8) This doll is expensive but I really like it.
9) I'm playing a wonderful game. Do you know it?
10) She's a fabulous gal. Do you know her?
11) The lessons are too difficult and we don't understand them.
12) I need some cigarettes and must buy them.
13) I know this woman although I don't like her.
14) Do you see them?
15) Do you want it for Monday?
16) She wears old clothes and she likes them.
17) They live in the rooms on top.
18) We only eat two meals a day.
19) The students often disappoint the teacher, but he likes them.
20) I'm taking the underground (US: subway). Are you taking it?
21) She only likes expensive bags; however, she never buys them.
22) Do you beat your wife from time to time? No, I never beat her.
23) I'm buying a house, but my guy doesn't like it.
24) The lesson's beginning. Do you find it very difficult?
25) The word is difficult. I can't write it.
26) The work is rather long. I don't want to do it.
27) The book is difficult, but I must finish it.
28) I like carrots. Do you like them?
29) I hate him, even though you are mad about him.
30) I know many interesting things. Do you know them?

VOCABULARIO

	traducción	sinónimo asociado	opuesto asociado
1. (la semana) próxima	next (week), following week	la semana siguiente, dentro de una semana = in a week	la semana pasada = last week
2. ¿a cuántos estamos hoy?	what's today's date?	estamos a . . . ; (la) fecha = the date	
3. necesitar	to need	hacer falta	faltar = to lack
4. /bromear/está bromeando	/to kid/you're kidding	(la) broma = joke	serio = serious
5. maravilloso	wonderful ≠ dreadful	fabuloso, único, fenomenal, estupendo, extraordinario, increíble, insólito, formidable, excepcional, brutal, fantástico	malísimo, horrible, horroroso, espantoso, terrible; así, así = so-so; regular, ordinario = ordinary, mediocre
6. jugar	to play	(el) juego = game; (el) juguete = toy; (la) muñeca = doll	
7. tonto	stupid, dumb ≠ intelligent	estúpido, bobo, idiota, cretino	inteligente, vivo, listo = clever
8. algo	something	alguna cosa = something; cualquier cosa = anything	nada = nothing
9. unas (unos)	some, a few	algunas(os) = unos pocos; todo = all	ninguno(a) = none
10. caer	to fall	to drop = dejar caer	recoger = to pick up
11. /¿cada cuánto? /¿desde cuándo?	/how often? /for how long?	¿desde hace cuánto tiempo?	
12. hermosa	beautiful (cute = mona)	guapa, bonita, linda, preciosa	feo = feucho = ugly
13. esta noche	tonight ≠ last night	(la) noche = evening	anoche, ayer por la noche mañana por la noche = tomorrow night

55

LECCIÓN 12

INDIRECT OBJECT PRONOUNS		
subject	*direct object*	*indirect object*
yo	**me**	**me (a mí)**
I	me	(to) me
tu	**te**	**te (a tí)**
you	you	(to) you
él/Vd.	**le**	**le (a él, Vd.)**
he, it	him, it	(to) him, you, it
ella/Vd.	**la**	**le (a ella, Vd.)**
she	her, it	(to) her, you
ello		
it		
nosotros(as)	**nos**	**nos (a nosotros(as))**
we	us	(to) us
vosotros(as)	**os**	**os (a vosotros(as))**
you	you	(to) you
ellos(as)/Vds.	**los/las/les**	**les (a ellos(as)/Vds.)**
they/you	them	(to) them, you

note: — These indirect pronouns don't exist in English and are a true
problem. Whenever 'to' is said or implied in English, they must be
used in Spanish.
— After some prepositions, mí, tí, él, ella, etc. are used for emphasis,
e.g. para mí = for me, para nosotros = for us, cerca de tí = near
you, sin ella = without her, con él = with him.
— conmigo = with me, consigo = with him, contigo = with you
— lo = things; le = to him, to her, to you; les = to them, to you

¿LE HABLA A MENUDO?	Do you often speak to him/her?
Sí, le hablo a menudo.	Yes, I often speak to him/her.
No, no le hablo a menudo.	No, I don't often speak to him/her.

note: 'le' may mean 'to him', 'to her' or 'to you'.

```
┌─────────────────────────────────────────────────────────────────────┐
│ POSITIVE                                                              │
│                                                                       │
│ Me hablo.                    I'm speaking to me.                      │
│ Te hablo.                    I'm speaking to you.                     │
│ Le hablo.                    I'm speaking to him/her/you.             │
│ Nos hablo.                   I'm speaking to us.                      │
│ Os hablo.                    I'm speaking to you.                     │
│ Les hablo.                   I'm speaking to them/you.                │
└─────────────────────────────────────────────────────────────────────┘
```

note: Hablo a mí = I'm speaking to myself. This can be used for emphasis.

```
┌─────────────────────────────────────────────────────────────────────┐
│ NEGATIVE                                                              │
│                                                                       │
│ No me hablo.                 I'm not speaking to me.                  │
│ No te hablo.                 I'm not speaking to you.                 │
│ No le hablo.                 I'm not speaking to him/her/you.         │
│ No nos hablo.                I'm not speaking to us.                   │
│ No os hablo.                 I'm not speaking to them/you.            │
│ No les hablo.                I'm not speaking to them/you.            │
└─────────────────────────────────────────────────────────────────────┘
```

CAREFUL!!

> **ATTACHED PRONOUNS**
>
> **No puedo mandarlo a ella.**   I can't send it to her.
> **Quiero dártelo**   I want to give it to you.
> **Intento entenderle.**   I'm trying to understand him/her /you.

note: — The direct and indirect object are attached to the infinitive.
       — 'le' becomes 'se' when there are two third-person pronouns, e.g. no puedo mandarselo = I can't send it to her

> **VERBS FOLLOWED BY A**
>
> | | | | |
> |---|---|---|---|
> | **dar a** | to give to | **ir a** | to go to |
> | **enseñar a** | to teach to | **esperar a** | to wait for |
> | **mostrar a** | to show to | **explicar a** | to explain to |
> | **mandar a** | to send to | **llamar a** | to call up |
> | **llevar a** | to bring to | **invitar a** | to invite |
> | **decir a** | to say | **escribir a** | to write to |
> | **querer a** | to love someone | **escuchar a** | to listen to |
>
> **Le escribo.**   I am writing to her/him/you.
> **Te espera.**   He's waiting for you.
> **Le da un libro.**   He's giving a book to her/him/you.
> **Nos explica el problema.**   She's explaining the problem to us.
> **Me escuchan.**   They're listening to me.
> **Les dice el problema.**   She's telling them/you the problem.

translate:

1) I know his mother, do you know her?
2) Fortunately, the maid does the housework.
3) She tells them all her problems.
4) He's giving her a pretty sweater. What are you giving her?
5) He often thinks of his wife.
6) I've been working for a long time. Are you still working?
7) Do you often speak to her? I hardly ever speak to her.
8) He is stupid, but in spite of that I like him.
9) I'm trying to understand you.
10) I love her and she loves me.
11) I've been waiting for you for two hours.
12) What are you bringing your relatives to eat?
13) Do you feel like showing your work to me?
14) We've been listening to that strange man for an hour.
15) We can't see them this evening.
16) His grandparents and his wife are giving him a new suit.
17) I don't want to tell them that he's crazy.
18) I don't like coffee; however, I'm used to drinking it.
19) He doesn't have to tell us his problems.
20) Go ahead, I'm listening to you.
21) For how long have you been teaching them Spanish?
22) Her in-laws have been waiting an hour for her.
23) I don't want to give it to you.
24) She's trying to bring him it.
25) That cute gal is calling him up again.
26) In spite of the weather, they are inviting us.
27) Even me, I like men a lot; above all, mine.
28) You don't have to call them up now.

VOCABULARIO

	traducción	sinónimo asociado	opuesto asociado
1. ni siquiera	not even		aún yo = incluso yo = even me
2. si	if	sí o no = whether or no	
3. (la) madre	mother ≠ father		(el) padre
4. (la) hermana	sister ≠ brother		(el) hermano
5. (la) suegra	mother-in-law ≠ father-in-law	(los) suegros = in-laws	(el) suegro
6. (la) sobrina	niece ≠ nephew	(la) tía = aunt; (el) tío = uncle; (el) primo = cousin	(el) sobrino
7. /(el) abuelo /(el) nieto	/grandfather /grandson	(los) nietos = grandchildren	(la) abuela = grandmother
8. (el) marido	husband ≠ wife	(el) esposo	(la) mujer
9. (el) hijo	son ≠ daughter	(los) padres = parents	(la) hija
10. soltero(a)	single ≠ married	novia(o) = engaged	casado
11. (la) familia	family	parientes = relatives	
12. (la) persona	person	(la) gente = people	
13. por ejemplo	for instance	(el) caso = case	
14. simpático	nice ≠ mean	agradable	malo, antipático
15. limpiar la casa	to do the housework	las faenas de la casa, (la) ama de casa = housewife	
16. durante	during	mientras = while (since = desde)	hasta = until
17. extraño	strange	raro, curioso	normal, natural
18. afortunada- mente	fortunately ≠ unfortunately	felizmente, por suerte = casualidad = luckily = por fortuna	desgraciadamente
19. (la) criada	maid	(la) asistenta	
20. tanto peor	too bad ≠ all the better	peor para (él)	tanto mejor

LECCIÓN 13

QUE	= WHO, WHICH, THAT (relative form)
La mujer que habla.	The woman who's talking.
El coche que está aquí.	The car which (that) is here.

¿QUIÉN(ES)?, ¿QUÉ?	= WHO?, WHAT? (interrogative form)
¿Quién?	Who?
¿Quién habla?	Who's speaking?
¿Quiénes son estos hombres?	Who are these men/women?
estas mujeres?	
¿Qué?	What?
¿Qué come?	What are you eating?

QUE	= THAT (conjunction)
¿Qué piensa?	What do you think?
Pienso que tiene razón.	I think (that) you are right.

note: — 'quiénes' = plural of 'who'.
 — in English the conjunctive 'that' is often omitted, but never in Spanish: the book you're looking for = el libro que buscas.

¿Qué es?	What is it?
¿Quién es?	Who is it?
¿Qué dices?	What are you saying?
¿Quién dice eso?	Who says that?
¿Qué buscas?	What are you looking for?
¿Quién te busca?	Who's looking for you?
¿A quién buscas?	Who are you looking for?
¿Quién habla?	Who is talking?
¿A quién habla?	Who are you talking to?

NUNCA	= NEVER, EVER
¿Fuma Vd. a veces?	Do you ever smoke?
Non, no fumo nunca.	No, I never smoke.

translate, then give the negative answer:

1) Do you ever take walks in the morning?
2) I never go to the cinema (US: movies) on Sundays.
3) Are you ever lucky?
4) We never understand the teacher.

CONOCER — TO KNOW —	**SABER**
(to be familiar with)	(to have knowledge)
conocer a alguien = to know someone	**saber algo** = to know something
conocer un sitio = to know a place	

note: sé conducir = I know how to drive.

¿Conoce	**París?**	Do you know	Paris?
	a̱ este hombre?		this man?
	este restaurante?		this restaurant?
¿Sabe	**inglés?**	Do you know	English?
	nadar?		how to swim?
	quién está aquí?		who is here?

translate:

1) Do you know Madrid?
2) Do you know how to drive?
3) Does she know his wife?
4) I don't know the answer.
5) Do you know his family?
6) Do you know how to swim?
7) Do you know Spanish?
8) Do you know this restaurant?
9) Does she know his relatives?
10) Do you know that?

62

translate:

1) I know you're right.
2) I think he's a nice guy.
3) Who are you looking at?
4) I think that he's successful.
5) I know that he needs money.
6) What is it?
7) Who is it?
8) Who are those women over there?
9) Who is she?
10) Who are those men?
11) Who are you talking to?
12) She thinks that I'm wrong.
13) He feels you're lucky.
14) What are you looking for?
15) Who's looking for me?
16) What are you drinking?
17) They don't feel you understand.
18) I agree he must do it.
19) I don't know what to say to him.
20) It seems to me the flat (US: apartment)'s too small.
21) Which flat (apartment)?
22) Which car do you want?
23) Which kind of meat do you want?
24) I don't know who she is.
25) I see the women who are in the street.
26) She knows who I love.
27) Which dog is yours.
28) You don't have to tell me that I'm wrong.

1)	**Estoy feliz** I'm happy	≠	**triste** sad
2)	**Enrique es grande** Harry's tall	≠	**pequeño** small
3)	**Es el mismo que el mío** It's the same as mine	≠	**diferente de** different from
4)	**El pastel está duro** The cake's hard	≠	**blando** soft
5)	**La ropa está seca** The laundry's dry	≠	**mojada** wet
6)	**Ha venido antes** He came before	≠	**despues** after
7)	**Un abrigo de piel es caro** A fur coat's expensive	≠	**barato** cheap
8)	**Este perro es valiente** This dog is brave	≠	**cobarde** cowardly
9)	**Estoy arriba** I'm upstairs	≠	**abajo** downstairs
10)	**Los cuartos de arriba** The rooms at the top	≠	**abajo** bottom
11)	**Mi coche es viejo** My car's old	≠	**nuevo** new
12)	**Mi contestación es verdadera** My answer's true	≠	**falsa** false
13)	**Trabajo media jornada** I work part-time	≠	**la jornada completa** full-time
14)	**Va muy arreglado** He wears formal clothes	≠	**deportivo** casual
15)	**La fiesta es muy formal/seria** The party's formal	≠	**sin formalismos** informal
16)	**No seas grosero** Don't be rude	≠	**educado** polite
17)	**Es esmerado en su trabajo** His work is careful	≠	**es descuidado en** careless
18)	**Está bien de fortuna/acomodado** He's well off	≠	**está pelado/sin blanca** broke
19)	**enseñar** to teach / **pedir prestado** to borrow / **cerrar** to close, shut	≠	**aprender** to learn / **prestar** to lend / **abrir** to open

VOCABULARIO

	traducción	sinónimo asociado	opuesto asociado
1. (el) cuarto de dormir	bedroom	(el) dormitorio; hacer la cama = to make one's bed	
2. /cuarto de estar /(el) comedor	/living room /dining room	(la) sala = drawing room = habitación	
3. (la) cocina	kitchen	(la) sartén = pan; (la) cazuela = pot	
4. /(el) cuarto de baño/(el) fregadero	/bathroom/sink	(el) lavabo = (el) retrete = WC, loo (US: john)	
5. /(la) moqueta /(las) cortinas	carpet, curtains	(la) alfombra = rug	
6. abajo	downstairs		arriba = upstairs
7. (el) piso	/apartment/floor	/apartamento /planta	
8. /(la) casa/(los) muebles	/house/furniture		
9. (el) suelo	ground	en el suelo = on the floor	
10. (la) lámpara	lamp	(la) bombilla = bulb, (la) luz = light	
11. /me siento bien /me parece que (no tienes razón)	/I feel good/I feel that (you're wrong)	me encuentro bien	
12. (la) calle	street	(el) camino, (la) carretera = road	
13. (el) ascensor	lift (US elevator)	(la) escalera = stairs	
14. cómodo	comfortable		incómodo = uncomfortable
15. depende de tí	it depends on you	como tu quieras = up to you	
16. ¡de prisa!	hurry up!	¡date prisa!; ¡corre!; ¡apresúrate!	listo = ready
17. (la) alacena	closet	(la) estantería = shelf	

LECCIÓN 14

PRESENT PARTICIPLE: **ESTAR + ANDO** = —ING

estoy			
estás			
está	hablando,	am	(in the midst of)
estamos	comiendo, etc.	are	speaking, eating, etc.
estáis			
están			

note: — To form the present participle, add 'ando' to the stem of the 'ar'
verbs, and 'iendo' to the 'er' and 'ir' verbs.
— hablo = I'm speaking; for slight increase of emphasis use 'estoy
hablando', e.g. estoy hablando desde hace dos horas = hablo desde
hace dos horas = I've been speaking for two hours.

¿ESTÁ COMIENDO?	Are you (in the midst of) eating?
Sí, estoy comiendo.	Yes, I'm eating.
No, no estoy comiendo.	No, I'm not eating.

66

```
CAREFUL!!

¿ESTÁ ESCRIBIENDO LA CARTA?     Are you          writing the letter?
                                Is he/she

Sí, estoy escribiendo la carta.     Yes, I'm writing the letter.
Sí, estoy escribiéndola.            Yes, I'm writing it.
```

note: As with the infinitive, you attach the object, whether direct or indirect.

translate:

1) Are your parents taking a trip now?
2) For the moment I'm working part-time.
3) He's still eating. He's been eating for two hours.
4) The letter? I'm writing it now.
5) The kids are playing.
6) They're all sleeping upstairs.
7) She's wearing the same coat as me.
8) You're teaching me Spanish and I'm learning.
9) We're going to a nice place.
10) I'm drinking it now.
11) She's calling him up.
12) I'm waiting for you.
13) They're listening to us.
14) Are they coming back now?
15) It's raining, it's snowing at the same time.
16) I'm beginning to do the work this week
17) What are they doing? They're walking.
18) They're laughing at me.
19) I'm closing the window.
20) She's telling it to him.
21) I'm giving it to her.
22) They're inviting us tonight.
23) She's explaining the problem to us.
24) I'm doing it now.

VERBOS IRREGULARES (present participle)

PRIMER GRUPO: AR

dar (to give)	→ **dando**	**pensar** (to think)	→ **pensando**
estar (to be)	→ **estando**	**despertar** (to wake up)	→ **despertando**
andar (to walk)	→ **andando**	**contar** (to count)	→ **contando**
empezar (to begin)	→ **empezando**	**acordar** (to remember)	→ **acordando**
sentar (to sit)	→ **sentando**	**jugar** (to play)	→ **jugando**
cerrar (to shut)	→ **cerrando**	**rogar** (to beg)	→ **rogando**

SECUNDO GRUPO: ER

valer (to be worth)	→ **valiendo**	**caber** (to contain)	→ **cabiendo**
ver (to see)	→ **viendo**	**soler** (to be used to)	→ **soliendo**
querer (to want)	→ **queriendo**	**volver** (to become)	→ **volviendo**
hacer (to make)	→ **haciendo**	**oler** (to smell)	→ **oliendo**
caer (to fall)	→ **cayendo**	**mover** (to move)	→ **moviendo**
saber (to know)	→ **sabiendo**	**entender** (to understand)	→ **entendiendo**
poner (to put)	→ **poniendo**	**conocer** (to know)	→ **conociendo**
proponer (to suggest)	→ **proponiendo**	**reconocer** (to recognise)	→ **reconociendo**
poder (can)	→ **pudiendo**	**parecer** (to seem)	→ **pareciendo**
ser (to be)	→ **siendo**	**pertenecer** (to belong to)	→ **perteneciendo**
tener (to have)	→ **teniendo**	**convencer** (to convince)	→ **convenciendo**
establecer (to set up)	→ **estableciendo**	**leer** (to read)	→ **leyendo**
nacer (to be born)	→ **naciendo**	**llover** (to rain)	→ **lloviendo**
proteger (to protect)	→ **protegiendo**	**coger** (to take)	→ **cogiendo**
traer (to bring)	→ **trayendo**	**doler** (to hurt)	→ **doliendo**
haber (to have)	→ **habiendo**	**creer** (to believe)	→ **creyendo**

TERCER GRUPO: IR

oír (to hear)	→ **oyendo**	**pedir** (to ask)	→ **pidiendo**
decir (to say)	→ **diciendo**	**conseguir** (to reach)	→ **consiguiendo**
venir (to come)	→ **viniendo**	**vestir** (to dress)	→ **vistiendo**
prevenir (to warn)	→ **previniendo**	**reñir** (to quarrel)	→ **riñendo**
convenir (to suit)	→ **conviniendo**	**concluir** (to conclude)	→ **concluyendo**
salir (to go)	→ **saliendo**	**huir** (to escape)	→ **huyendo**
dormir (to sleep)	→ **durmiendo**	**construir** (to build)	→ **construyendo**
morir (to die)	→ **muriendo**	**conducir** (to drive)	→ **conduciendo**
sentir (to feel)	→ **sintiendo**	**elegir** (to choose)	→ **eligiendo**
preferir (to prefer)	→ **prefiriendo**	**reir** (to laugh)	→ **riendo**
divertir (to enjoy)	→ **divirtiendo**	**desvestirse** (to undress)	→ **desvistiendo**
repetir (to repeat)	→ **repitiendo**	**servir** (to serve)	→ **sirviendo**
seguir (to follow)	→ **siguiendo**	**distinguir** (to distinguish)	→ **distinguiendo**

VOCABULARIO

	traducción	sinónimo asociado	opuesto asociado
1. /bueno/mejor /el mejor	good, better, the best		/malo/peor/el peor = /bad/worse/the worst
2. /viajar/(el) viaje /(el) agente de viajes	/to travel/a trip /a travel agent	hacer (dar) un viaje = to take a trip; (la) temporada = stay	
3. (el) billete de ida	single (US: one-way) ticket ≠ return (US: round trip)	(el) boleto	uno de ida y vuelta
4. reservar	to reserve ≠ to cancel	completo = booked	anular
5. /(la) ciudad/(el) pueblo	/city/village	(la) aldea, (el) país = country	
6. de vacaciones	on holiday	(el) hotel = hotel	
7. /(la) playa/(el) mar/(el) traje de baño	/beach/sea/bathing suit	a orillas del mar = seaside; (la) arena = sand; nadar = to swim; (la) piscina = pool	
8. /(la) montaña /en el campo	/mountain/in the country	(la) sierra; esquiar = to ski	(el) valle = valley
9. estoy a favor de	I'm for ≠ against		en contra de
10. (el) dinero	money (dollar = (el) dólar)	(la) pasta = dough; (la) vuelta = cambio = (el) suelto = change	líquido = especie = (en) metalico = cash
11. /(el) cheque/(el) banco	/cheque (US: check) /bank		
12. (el) aparato de fotos	camera ((la) foto = photo)	(la) máquina de fotografía, (la) película = film	
13. (el) sitio	place	(el) lugar	
14. /(la) ducha/(el) baño	/shower/bath	(la) bañera = bathtub	
15. (la) quemadura del sol	sunburn	(el) bronceado = tan; tomar el sol = sunbathe	

69

LECCIÓN 15

PUBLIC ENEMY NUMBER ONE!!!

I've been working for an hour.	**Trabajo desde hace una hora.**
	Estoy trabajando desde hace una hora.
	Hace una hora que trabajo.
compare:	
	Comemos desde hace dos horas.
We've been eating for two hours.	**Estamos comiendo desde hace dos horas.**
	Hace dos horas que comemos.
	Están viviendo aquí desde hace diez años.
They've lived here for ten years.	**Hace diez años que están viviendo aquí.**
	Vivien aquí desde hace diez años.

¿HACE CUÁNTO TIEMPO QUE ESPERA?	For how long have you been waiting?
Espero desde hace una hora.	
Hace una hora que espero.	I've been waiting for an hour.
Estoy esperando desde hace una hora.	

note: ¿Desde hace cuánto tiempo? = ¿Hace cuánto tiempo?

ENGLISH PAST WHICH   =   PRESENT in Spanish
CONTINUES!

Trabaja aquí desde hace cinco años?	Have you been working here for five years?
Sí, trabajo aquí desde hace cinco años.	Yes, I've been working here for five years.
No, no trabajo aquí desde hace cinco años.	No, I haven't been working here for five years.

DESDE = SINCE
a definite point in time
(date)

DESDE HACE = FOR
a certain length of time

estoy casada = I've been married

desde el mes de julio	**desde hace dos meses**
since July	for two months
desde el año pasado	**desde hace diez años**
since last year	for ten years

learn the ordinal numbers:

first =   **primero**
second = **segundo**
third =   **tercero**
fourth =   **cuarto**
fifth =   **quinto**

translate:

1) Hace cinco años que estudio español.
2) ¿Hace cuánto tiempo que Vd. le quiere?
3) Según él, están aquí desde el verano.
4) Vd. está trabajando desde esta mañana.
5) ¿Hace cuánto tiempo que están casados?
6) Trabajamos juntos desde hace dos meses.
7) Estamos construyendo nuestra casa desde el otoño.
8) Te espera desde hace una hora.
9) Está escribiendole desde hace mucho.
10) Viven juntos desde la primavera pasada.
11) ¿Están aquí desde hace dos horas?
12) Estoy escuchándole desde hace diez minutos.
13) Intento ayudarle desde el año pasado.
14) Hace diez años que les conozco.

translate:

1) For how long have you been here?
2) We've been eating for an hour.
3) They've been living in their new house since the summer
4) For how long have you been working here?
5) We've been walking for an hour.
6) He's been married to her since the summer.
7) For how long has he been sick?
8) I've been divorced for a year.
9) I've been trying to understand you since the beginning.
10) I've had to work with him for five years.
11) For how long have you been living together?
12) The book? I've been writing it for a year.
13) For how long have you known her?
14) I've been trying to sell my car for six months.

ADVERBIOS Y FRASES 3

1. **cuanto antes mejor**	the sooner the better	14. — **reciente- mente**	— recently
2. **el día siguiente**	the next day	— **no hace mucho**	— not long ago
3. **el día antes**	the day before	15. — **sólo**	— only
4. **durante**	during	— **solamente**	
5. **¿cada cuánto?**	how often?	— **no tengo más que**	— I only have
6. **por termino medio**	on the average	16. **cada dos semanas**	every other week
7. **por encima de todo**	above all	17. — **tan pronto** — **luego que**	as soon as
8. — **por si acaso** — **en caso que**	just in case, in case	18. — **adrede, a posta** — **a propósito**	on purpose
9. **pronto**	soon	19. **en cuanto a**	as far as
10. **a mediados de**	in the middle of	20. **varios**	several
11. **según**	according to	21. — **además de** — **qué más**	— besides — what more?, — what else?
12. — **a partir de** — **del** — **en adelante**	as of . . . from on	22. — **en conjunto** — **en general** — **la mayoría de**	— on the whole — in general — most of
13. — **dado que** — **como** — **puesto que** — **ya que**	given that, since	23. **con respecto a**	as for
		24. **en la medida en que**	in so far as
		25. **a propósito de**	concerning

VOCABULARIO

	traducción	sinónimo asociado	opuesto asociado
1. está tireado	it's a cinch ≠ hard	es cosa facíl	difícil = rough
2. tiene razón	you're right ≠ wrong		se equivoca
3. dejar de	to stop ≠ start, begin	parar, detener	empezar, comenzar, principiar, seguir, continuar = to go on
4. nervioso	nervous, tense	tenso	tranquilo, sereno
5. falso	false ≠ true	falsificado, engañoso = fake	verdadero
6. entonces	then, so	pues, luego, así	
7. tirar	to throw ≠ catch	echar	coger
8. ganador	winner ≠ loser	ganar = to win	perdedor, perder = to lose
9. ¿y qué?	so what?	¿así qué?	ya sabes = you know very well
10. (la) falta	mistake	(el) error	
11. comprar	to buy ≠ sell	vendedor = salesman	vender
12. este mismo día	this very day		
13. /(el) pasatiempo favorito/(el) fan	/hobby/fan	(la) actividad favorita, (el) seguidor, (el) aficionado	
14. poner	to put	meter = to put in; ponerse = to put on	
15. /Navidad /Pascua	/Christmas/Easter	Noche Buena, Noche Vieja = New Year's Eve	
16. escoger	to choose, select	elegir, seleccionar, decidir = decide	
17. justo	fair ≠ unfair		injusto
18. estar preocupado	to be worried, upset	preocupaciones = worries	no te preocupes = don't worry
19. de todas maneras	in any case	de todas formas, en todo caso	
20. ayudar	to help		

LECCIÓN 16

TIEMPO FUTURO (future)

hablaré	I'll speak
hablarás	you'll speak
hablará	he/she/you'll speak
hablaremos	we'll speak
hablaréis	you'll speak
hablarán	they'll speak

note: This tense is extremely easy: just add the above endings to the infinitive.

¿LE HABLARÁ mañana? / la semana próxima? / dentro de una semana?   Will you speak with him tomorrow? / next week? / in a week?

Sí, le hablaré mañana.   Yes, I'll speak with him tomorrow.
No, no le hablaré mañana.   No, I won't speak with him tomorrow.

translate:

1) ¿Verá a su novio la semana próxima?
2) ¿Sabes si nos auydará de todas formas?
3) Dejaremos de trabajar dentro de una hora.
4) Tendremos hambre pronto.
5) ¿No sé si vendrá con nosotros?
6) Dice que no comprará otro coche igual.
7) Ni siquiera saben si podremos hacerlo o no.
8) Este chisme valdrá mucho dinero dentro de algunos años.
9) ¿Te lo dirá mañana?
10) ¿Hará un viaje el verano próximo?
11) ¿Saldrán Vds. esta tarde?
12) Tendremos que decírselo mañana.
13) Llevaré mi traje nuevo esta noche.
14) Me llamarás dentro de una hora?

translate:

1) I'll be at home this afternoon.
2) Will you need more money?
3) I'll call you tonight in any case.
4) We'll go for a walk in spite of the bad weather.
5) I'll be able to do it next week.
6) You'll have to ask him this evening.
7) She'll drink a lot of wine tonight.
8) You'll catch cold because of the rain.
9) I'll be ready at ten.
10) He'll need a pill for his headache.
11) I'm sure you'll be lucky.
12) You'll get used to it soon.
13) I'll bring him with me this afternoon.

VERBOS IRREGULARES (futuro)

There are no irregularities in verbs of the first group (AR).

SEGUNDO GRUPO: ER

VALER = to be worth
valdré

QUERER = to want
querré

HACER = to make
haré

SABER = to know
sabré

PONER = to put
pondré

PROPONER = to suggest
propondré

PODER = to be able to
podré

TENER = to have
tendré

HABER = to have
habré

CABER = to contain
cabré

TERCER GRUPO: IR

DECIR = to say
diré

VENIR = to come
vendré

PREVENIR = to warn
prevendré

CONVENIR = to suit
convendré

SALIR = to go out
saldré

VOCABULARIO

	traducción	sinónimo asociado	opuesto asociado
1. cansado	tired, beat	reventado, deshecho molido, muerto	estar muy bien = to feel great
2. estar enfermo	to be ill ≠ well, (la) salud = health	estar malo	estar mejor = to feel better
3. estornudar	to sneeze	¡Jesús! = Bless you!	
4. tener un catarro	to catch a cold	tener gripe = flu, fiebre = fever	
5. (la) medicina	medicine	(el) comprimido = tablet, (la) píldora = pill	
6. toser	to cough	(el) dolor de garganta = sore throat	
7. (el) dentista	dentist	(los) dientes	
8. /(el) dolor de cabeza/de estómago	headache, stomach ache		
9. me duele, ¿le duele?	it hurts, does it hurt?	¿tiene dolor?, (el) dolor	
10. listo	/ready/clever		
11. pasar	/to happen/to pass	llegar = tener; lugar = to take place = ocurrir = suceder	
12. llevar	/to carry/to wear	traer = to bring	
13. para que	so that	a fin de que	
14. reir	to laugh ≠ to cry	(la) sonrisa = smile	llorar; (la) lágrima = tear
15. tener buena cara	to look well	parecer bien	
16. el mismo que	the same as ≠ different from	semejante a = igual que = similar to; algo así = something like that	diferente de, opuesto
17. por todas partes	everywhere ≠ nowhere	en todas partes	en ninguna parte, en ningún sitio
18. (el) canalla	bastard	(el) marrano = louse; (el) cerdo, (el) puerco, (el) sinvergüenza; asqueroso = lousy	(la) perra = bitch

LECCIÓN 17

> **SI** = IF (conditional 1)
>
> **¿SI TIENE DINERO, COMPRARÁ**   If you have the money, will you
> **UN COCHE?**   buy a car?
>
>   present   +   future
>
> **Sí, si tengo dinero, compraré un**   Yes, if I have the money, I'll buy
> **coche.**   a car.
> **No, si tengo dinero, no compraré**   No, if I have the money, I won't
> **un coche.**   buy a car.

note: There's nothing particularly difficult about this structure, which is the same in both languages.

translate and then give the affirmative answer:

1) ¿Si está cansado, irá a la cama?
2) ¿Si le duele la garganta, tomará un comprimido?
3) ¿Si tiene un catarro, estará cansada?
4) ¿Si me pregunta Vd. algo, le contestaré?
5) ¿Si puede hacerlo sola, lo hará?
6) ¿Si me llamas, contestaré?
7) ¿Si un amigo tiene que ir al médico, iré con el?
8) ¿Si tengo hambre, me darás algo de comer?
9) ¿Si hace buen tiempo, iremos al cine?
10) ¿Si tiene dinero, comprará una casa nueva?

translate and then give the negative answer:

1) If you need help, will you call me?
2) If they lose weight, will they feel better?
3) If she has a lot of money, will she buy a new apartment?
4) If I'm sick, will you go with me to the doctor?
5) If I must take a trip next week, will you come with me?
6) If he's lucky, will he win a lot of money?
7) If you wife loves me, will you be happy?
8) If they don't understand, will the teacher help them?
9) If you can't do it, will you tell me?
10) If the boss is wrong, will we know?
11) If you aren't used to drinking, will you be sick?
12) If the restaurant's expensive, will we go in any case?

1)	**querer** to love	≠	**odiar** to hate
2)	**ponerse de pie, levantarse** to stand up	≠	**sentarse** to sit down
3)	**vestirse** to dress	≠	**desvestirse** to undress
4)	**ir de prisa** to hurry up	≠	**tomar su tiempo** to take one's time
5)	**volver** to come back	≠	**partir/salir** to go away/out
6)	**encontrar** to find	≠	**perder** to lose
7)	**olvidar** to forget	≠	**acordarse/recordar** to remember
8)	**comprar** to buy	≠	**vender** to sell
9)	**ganar** to win	≠	**perder** to lose
10)	**ponerse (el abrigo)** to put on (coat)	≠	**quitar** to take off
11)	**estar de acuerdo con** to agree with	≠	**estar en desacuerdo con** to disagree with
12)	**aterrizar** to land	≠	**despegar** to take off
13)	**poner/encender** to put on, turn on	≠	**apagar** to put off
14)	**dormirse** to fall asleep	≠	**despertarse** to wake up
15)	**prestar atención a** to pay attention	≠	**no tomar en cuenta** to ignore
16)	**preguntar** to ask	≠	**contestar** to answer
17)	**empujar/dar** to push/to give	≠	**tirar/tomar** to pull/to take
18)	**reir** to laugh	≠	**llorar** to cry
19)	**bajar** to go down	≠	**subir** to go up
20)	**salir/estar (en casa)** to go out/be in	≠	**quedarse/no estar /en casa)** to stay in/be out

VOCABULARIO

	traducción	sinónimo asociado	opuesto asociado
1. llamar por teléfono	to call up	telefonear; (el) telefonazo = telephone call	
2. colgar	to hang up ≠ to pick up		descolgar
3. ¡no cuelgue!	hold on!	¡no se retire!	
4. ¿quién llama?	who's speaking?	¿quién es?, ¿de parte de quién?	Señor . . . llamando = on the line
5. ahora mismo se pone	I'll put you through to . . .	le paso . . . ; le pongo con . . .	
6. estoy ocupado	I'm busy ≠ free	estoy atareado	libre
7. como quiera	as you like	como desee; como gusta	
8. /alguien/cualquiera	/someone/anyone, whoever ≠ no one	no importa quien, todo el mundo = everyone	nadie
9. /(una) historia /(la) novela/(el) escritor	/story/novel/writer	novela corta = short stories, ficción = fiction	
10. gracioso	funny ≠ a drag	divertido, entretenido	aburrido, pesado
11. (el) amigo	friend ≠ enemy	amiguete = pal, compañero	enemigo
12. dos semanas	fortnight	(la) quincena	
13. con motivo de	on account of	por, a causa de, debido a = due to	¿por qué? = why?
14. perezoso	lazy ≠ hard-working	(el) holgazán, (el) vago = lazybones	trabajador
15. me quedan dos	I have two left ≠ I need two	restan dos = two are left	me hacen falta dos; no me queda = I don't have any left
16. intentar	to try	probar, tratar de	
17. (la) cita (dar)	an appointment (to make an . . .)	citar a alguien	
18. ¡he aquí . . . !	here is, are	¡he ahí!, tén!, toma!	
19. sin embargo	however	no obstante, aunque = although	

LECCIÓN 18

THE COMPARATIVE FORM	
joven	young
más joven	younger
el/la más joven	youngest

note: bueno, mejor, el/la mejor = good, better, best
malo, peor, el/la peor = bad, worse, worst
grande, mayor, el/la mayor = big, bigger, biggest
pequeño, menor, el/la menor = small, smaller, smallest

Es más joven que yo.	He's younger than me.
Es tan joven como yo.	He's as young as me.
No es tan joven como yo.	He isn't as young as me.
Es menos inteligente que yo.	He's less intelligent than me.

note: mucho más = much more.

translate and give the five possible forms:
e.g. joven, más joven que, menos joven que, el/la más joven que, tan joven como

1)	long	11)	safe	21)	deep
2)	bad	12)	far	22)	weak
3)	sweet	13)	sad	23)	pretty
4)	hot	14)	heavy	24)	dangerous
5)	thin	15)	cheap	25)	interesting
6)	strong	16)	bright, intelligent	26)	boring
7)	serious	17)	expensive	27)	polite
8)	fair	18)	old	28)	good
9)	beautiful	19)	crazy	29)	stupid
10)	sloppy	20)	crowded	30)	full

put in the superlative form:

1) Es . . . (grande) de la familia.
2) Este aparato de foto es . . . (bueno) de la tienda.
3) Mi vestido es . . . (bonito).
4) Este banco es . . . (limpio) de la ciudad.
5) Esta región es . . . (pobre) de Europa.
6) La moneda francesa es . . . (bonito).
7) Estas montañas son . . . (difíciles) de subir.
8) Ese panadero es . . . (caro).
9) Es el regalo . . . (precioso) que tengo.
10) Su sortija es . . . (maravilloso) de la joyería.
11) Este supermercado es . . . (cercano) a casa.
12) Tu pulsera es . . . (grande) de todas.
13) Este negocio es . . . (bueno) del año.
14) Este carnicero es . . . (malo) de la calle.

put in the comparative form:

1) Esta chica es . . . (serio) . . . yo.
2) Esta playa es . . . (bonito) . . . esa.
3) El primer piso está . . . (limpio) . . . el de abajo.
4) El panadero está . . . (cerca) . . . carnicero.
5) Su sortija es . . . (caro) . . . mi pulsera.
6) Su mujer es . . . (feo) . . . la suya.
7) Esta película es . . . (malo) . . . la de ayer.
8) Mi hermana es . . . (simpático) . . . su novio.
9) Esta lección es . . . (interesante) . . . la otra.
10) Es . . . (guapo) . . . su mujer.
11) Su nueva novela es . . . (bueno) . . . la primera.
12) Este juego es . . . (aburrido) . . . el otro.
13) Su hija es . . . (gracioso) . . . su mujer.
14) Este trabajo es . . . (importante) . . . el de la semana pasada.

translate and then put in the comparative form:
e.g. He works as hard as I do.
— Trabaja tan duro como yo.
— Trabaja más duro que yo.

1) She's as pretty as your sister.
2) Our trip is as interesting as yours.
3) My shoes are as cheap as theirs.
4) Your jewellery is as beautiful as hers.
5) This book is as crummy as that one.
6) Your hobby is as boring as mine.
7) The director is as bad as his play.
8) This lesson's as easy as the last one.
9) Your wallet is as full as mine.
10) This novel is as horrible as the last one.
11) That play is as good as the book.
12) My shower is as hot as Jane's.
13) My money is as good as yours.
14) Their homework is as difficult as ours.
15) His sister-in-law is as cute as her mother.
16) My bathing-suit is as pretty as my cousin's.
17) This restaurant is as crowded as the other one.
18) My room is as sloppy as yours.
19) My dress is as charming as yours.
20) He's as lazy as his father.
21) They're as well off as their parents.
22) I'm as poor as you are.
23) The teachers are as silly as the students.
24) Their apartment is as high as my house.
25) My pals are as funny as yours.
26) These mountains are as high as a skyscraper.

```
┌─────────────────────────────────────────────────────────────────┐
│  TANTO(S) ... COMO            =   AS MUCH AS, AS MANY AS          │
│                                                                   │
│  Tengo tanto dinero como Vd.      I have as much money as you.    │
│  Tengo tantos problemas como Vd.  I have as many problems as you. │
│  No tengo tanta prisa como él.    I am not as much in a hurry as he is. │
└─────────────────────────────────────────────────────────────────┘
```

note: — tan + adjective and adverb.
       — tanto + noun.

```
┌─────────────────────────────────────────────────────────────────┐
│  ADVERB = ADJECTIVE + —MENTE                                      │
│                                                                   │
│  probable   →   probablemente                                     │
│  posible    →   posiblemente                                      │
│  fácil      →   facilmente                                        │
│  seguro     →   seguramente                                       │
└─────────────────────────────────────────────────────────────────┘
```

note: Although the adverb is usually formed by adding 'mente' to the adjective (feminine form), exceptions are: despacio, pronto.

translate and then put into the adverb form:

1) sad	12) fast
2) difficult	13) funny
3) good	14) happy
4) bad	15) dry
5) serious	16) rare
6) easy	17) stupid
7) slow	18) intelligent
8) long	19) all of a sudden
9) frequent	20) crazy
10) soft	21) immediately
11) deep	22) glad
	23) marvellous

85

```
┌─────────────────────────────────────────────────────────────────┐
│  ALGUIEN ≠ NADIE          =   SOMEONE ≠ NO ONE                    │
│                                                                   │
│  ¿Ve Vd. a alguien?           Do you see someone?                 │
│  Sí, veo a alguien.           Yes, I see someone.                 │
│  No, no veo a nadie.          No, I don't see anyone.             │
└─────────────────────────────────────────────────────────────────┘
```

```
┌─────────────────────────────────────────────────────────────────┐
│  ALGO ≠ NADA              =   SOMETHING ≠ ANYTHING                │
│                                                                   │
│  ¿Tiene Vd. algo?             Do you have something?              │
│  Sí, tengo algo.              Yes, I have something.              │
│  No, no tengo nada.           No, I haven't anything.             │
└─────────────────────────────────────────────────────────────────┘
```

translate and then answer in the negative:

1) Have you something to do tonight?
2) Are you going somewhere after the lesson?
3) Is there someone important in the room?
4) Will you go anywhere with me?
5) Will she give me something to drink?
6) Will they see anything interesting at the cinema (US: movies)?
7) Can you find something amusing to do this evening?
8) Is someone here a sexy broad?
9) Is there something worse than a bad cop?
10) Will you do something exciting this afternoon?
11) Is anyone going to see you after the lesson?
12) Are you going somewhere alone?
13) Is anyone here rich?
14) Will you see him somewhere in New York?

VOCABULARIO

	traducción	sinónimo asociado	opuesto asociado
1. /(el) regalo /regalar	/a gift, present /to give	(el) presente; (la) sorpresa = surprise	
2. importante	important ≠ beside the point	notable	fuera de tema
3. ¿qué medida?	what size?	¿qué talle? (in clothing)	
4. el primer piso	first floor	planta baja = ground floor	
5. rebajas	sales	(la) liquidación, (la) ganga = bargain	
6. /ultramarinos /(el) panadero /(el) carnicero	/grocery/baker /butcher	(el) supermercado = supermarket	
7. lo esperaba	I expected it	no me extranaría = it wouldn't surprise me; lo sospechaba = me lo figuraba = I thought as much	inesperado = unexpected; icon razón = no wonder!
8. rico	rich ≠ poor	desahogado, acomodado = well off	pobre, pelado = sin blanca = broke
9. vale la pena	it's worth it ≠ not worth it	merece la pena	no vale la pena; no hace falta = it is not necessary
10. (la) cantidad	amount	suma, total	
11. ¡diablos!	goodness!, Heavens!	¡cómo!, ¡hombre!, ¡ay!, ¡diantres!, ¡Dios mío!, ¡Jesús!, ¡qué barbaridad!, ¡qué rabia!, ¡vaya!	gracias a Dios! = thank goodness!
12. ¿cuántos años tiene?	how old are you?	(la) edad = age, (la) juventud = youth	(la) vejez = old age
13. (la) joyería	jewellery	(la) sortija = ring, (la) pulsera = bracelet, (el) collar = necklace, (el) pendiente = earring	
14. (la) tienda	store	(el) almacén	

LECCIÓN 19

PRETÉRITO INDICATIVO (past — specific time)

AR		ER — IR	
hablé	hablamos	aprendí	aprendimos
hablaste	hablásteis	aprendiste	aprendísteis
habló	hablaron	aprendió	aprendieron

note: — The above endings are added to the stem.
— This past tense is used for a finished action within a <u>specific</u> time.

<u>Ayer</u>			yesterday.
<u>La semana pasada</u>	acabé mi libro.	I finished my book	<u>last week</u>.
<u>Hace</u> dos días			two days ago.

¿LE HABLASTE AYER?	Did you speak to him yesterday?
Sí, ayer le hablé.	Yes, I spoke with him yesterday.
No, ayer no le hablé.	No, I didn't speak with him yesterday.

revision:

No habló **más.**	He didn't speak any more.
No habló con **nadie.**	He didn't speak to anyone.
No habló **nunca.**	He never spoke.
No tuvo **nada.**	He had nothing.
No tuvo **más que** un coche.	He had only a car.
No vino **todavía.**	He hasn't come yet.

SER		**ESTAR**	
fui	fuimos	estuve	estuvimos
fuiste	fuísteis	estuviste	estuvísteis
fue	fueron	estuvo	estuvieron

TENER		**HABER**	
tuve	tuvimos	hube	hubimos
tuviste	tuvísteis	hubiste	hubísteis
tuvo	tuvieron	hubo	hubieron

translate and then give the negative answer:

1) Did he leave his office at ten?
2) Did they go for a walk last Sunday?
3) Did she catch a cold in the snow?
4) Did you sneeze a little while ago?
5) Did your teeth ache last week?
6) Did that happen yesterday?
7) Did you have a sore throat two weeks ago?
8) Did she rest after her work yesterday?
9) Did you bring the books along?
10) Was the play successful last week?
11) Was she lucky with you?
12) Did you have to go yesterday?
13) Were you afraid of the dogs?
14) Were you twenty-five last month?
15) Did you live there a long time?
16) Did you like their wedding a month ago?
17) Did the plane take off on time?
18) Did you do it with your husband last week?
19) Did she wear a new coat yesterday?
20) Did they tell you what they knew two days ago?
21) Did they finish their lesson last night?
22) Did you hear what she said?
23) Did you think that he went with her?
24) Did she buy that skirt in that store the other day?
25) Did we have to go out last night?
26) Did she have to go so soon?
27) Did they send you the books on time?
28) Did you hate your parents when they divorced?

translate and give the 'yo' and 'nosotros' forms:
e.g. to give
— dar, di, dimos

1)	to make	17)	to think	34)	to want
2)	to come back	18)	to be used to	35)	to begin
3)	to remember	19)	to drive	36)	to love
4)	to reach	20)	to go	37)	to serve
5)	to come	21)	to say	38)	to return
6)	to cook	22)	to count	39)	to seem
7)	to smell	23)	to give	40)	to recognise
8)	to be (2 forms)	24)	to bring	41)	to move
9)	to sleep	25)	to see	42)	to wake up
10)	to ask	26)	to choose	43)	to fall
11)	to have (2)	27)	to hear	44)	to quarrel
12)	to follow	28)	to rain	45)	to be worth
13)	to play	29)	to read	46)	to die
14)	to escape	30)	to understand	47)	to feel
15)	to be born	31)	to walk	48)	to laugh
16)	to know (2)	32)	to suggest	49)	to prefer
		33)	to promise	50)	to conclude

VERBOS IRREGULARES DE PRIMER GRUPO: AR (pretérito indicativo)

DAR = to give
dí
dió
dimos
dieron

ESTAR = to be
estuve
estuvo
estuvimos
estuvieron

ANDAR = to walk
anduve
anduvo
anduvimos
anduvieron

EMPEZAR = to begin
empecé
empezó
empezamos
empezaron

SENTAR(SE) = to sit
senté
sentó
sentamos
sentaron

CERRAR = to shut
cerré
cerró
cerramos
cerraron

PENSAR = to think
pensé
pensó
pensamos
pensaron

DESPERTAR = to wake up
desperté
despertó
despertamos
despertaron

CONTAR = to count
conté
contó
contamos
contaron

ACORDAR(SE) = to remember
acordé
acordó
acordamos
acordaron

JUGAR = to play
jugué
jugó
jugamos
jugaron

ROGAR = to beg
rogué
rogó
rogamos
rogaron

VERBOS IRREGULARES DE SEGUNDO GRUPO: <u>ER</u> (pretérito indicativo)

VALER = to be worth
valí
valió
valimos
valieron

VER = to see
ví
vió
vimos
vieron

QUERER = to want
quise
quiso
quisimos
quisieron

HACER = to make
hice
hizo
hicimos
hicieron

TRAER = to bring
traje
trajo
trajimos
trajeron

CAER = to fall
caí
cayó
caímos
cayeron

SABER = to know
supe
supo
supimos
supieron

PONER = to put
puse
puso
pusimos
pusieron

PROPONER = to suggest
propose
propuso
propusimos
propusieron

PODER = can
pude
pudo
pudimos
pudieron

SER = to be
fui
fue
fuimos
fueron

TENER = to have
tuve
tuvo
tuvimos
tuvieron

HABER = to have
hube
hubo
hubimos
hubieron

CABER = to contain
cupe
cupo
cupimos
cupieron

SOLER = to be used to
solí
solió
solimos
solieron

VOLVER = to become
volví
volvió
volvimos
volvieron

OLER = to smell
olí
olió
olimos
olieron

MOVER = move
moví
movió
movimos
movieron

ENTENDER = to understand
entendí
entendió
entendimos
entendieron

CONOCER = to know
conocí
conoció
conocimos
conocieron

PERTENECER = to belong
pertenecí
perteneció
pertenecimos
pertenecieron

RECONOCER = to recognise
reconocí
reconoció
reconocimos
reconocieron

PARECER = to seem
parecí
pareció
parecimos
parecieron

CONVENCER = to convince
convencí
convenció
convencimos
convencieron

ESTABLECER = to set up
establecí
estableció
establecimos
establecieron

LEER = to read
leí
leyó
leimos
leyeron

DOLER = to hurt
dolí
dolió
dolimos
dolieron

NACER = to be born
nací
nació
nacimos
nacieron

LLOVER = to rain
llovió

PROTEGER = to protect
protegí
protegió
protegimos
protegieron

COGER = to take
cogí
cogió
cogimos
cogieron

VERBOS IRREGULARES DE TERCER GRUPO: IR (pretérito indicativo)

VENIR = to come
vine
vino
vinimos
vinieron

OÍR = to hear
oí
oyó
oimos
oyeron

DECIR = to say
dije
dijo
dijimos
dijeron

REPETIR = to repeat
repetí
repitió
repetimos
repitieron

PREVENIR = to warn
previne
previno
previnimos
previnieron

DIVERTIR(SE) = to enjoy
divertí
divertió
divertimos
divirtieron

CONSEGUIR =to reach
conseguí
consiguió
conseguimos
consiguieron

SEGUIR = to follow
seguí
siguió
seguimos
signieron

PEDIR = to ask
pedí
pidió
pedimos
pidieron

SENTIR = to feel
sentí
sintió
sentimos
sintieron

VESTIR(SE) = to dress
vestí
vistió
vestimos
vistieron

REÑIR = to quarrel
reñí
riñó
reñimos
riñeron

CONCLUIR = to conclude
concluí
concluyó
concluimos
concluyeron

CONDUCIR = to drive
conduje
condujo
condujimos
condujeron

DESVERTIRSE = to undress
desvestí
desvistió
desvestimos
desvistieron

SALIR = to go
salí
salió
salimos
salieron

HUIR = to escape
huí
huyó
huimos
huyeron

DISTINGUIR = to distinguish
distinguí
distinguió
distinguimos
distinguieron

SERVIR = to serve
serví
sirvió
servimos
sirvieron

DORMIR = to sleep
dormí
durmió
dormimos
dumieron

PREFERIR = to prefer
preferí
prefirió
preferimos
prefirieron

CONSTRUIR = to build
construí
construyó
construimos
construyeron

ELEGIR = to choose
elegí
eligió
elegimos
eligieron

CONVENIR = to suit
convine
convino
convinimos
convinieron

MORIR = to die
morí
murió
morimos
murieron

REIR = to laugh
reí
rió
reimos
rieron

94

VOCABULARIO

	traducción	sinónimo asociado	opuesto asociado
1. probable	likely ≠ unlikely	muy posible, probablemente = most likely	improbable
2. /(el) colegio/(el) liceo/(la) clase /(el) curso	/school/secondary (US high) school /class, form (US grade)/course (US class)	(la) universidad = university, college, (la) clase = classroom, (la) nota = mark	
3. necessario		es una obligación, es un compromiso = it's a must	innecesario, opcional = optional
4. (el) diploma	diploma	(el) título, titulado = graduated	
5. tener éxito	to be successful ≠ to fail		fracasar, fallar
6. (el) éxito	a hit ≠ failure	(el) acierto	(el) fracaso
7. muy	very	completamente = del todo, absolutamente mucho, muchísimo; más o menos = more or less	bastante = rather = más bien, casi = almost, apenas = hardly, no del todo mal = not bad
8. preferido	favourite	favorito	
9. casarse	to get married	la luna de miel = honeymoon	divorciarse = to get divorced
10. matrimonio	marriage	(la) boda = wedding	divorcio
11. visitar	to sightsee	hacer una visita = to visit someone	
12. pertenecer	to belong to	ser de uno, poseer	
13. mi propio . . .	my own . . .	el mío = mine	
14. (el) turista	tourist	(el) arte = art; (la) iglesia = church; (el) monumento = monument	
15. todo derecho	straight ahead	siga recto, todo seguido	
16. a la derecha	to the right ≠ to the left	doblar = to turn	a la izquierda
17. ¡cállate!	keep quiet!	¡cierra el pico! = shut up!	
18. es lo mismo	it's the same thing	es igual, es la misma cosa	

LECCIÓN 20

IMPERFECTO ≠ (imperfect) = WAS + —ING

MIRABA LA TELE
{ **MIENTRAS LEÍA.**
{ **CUANDO ENTRÓ.**

I was watching TV
(was in the midst of)
{ while he was reading.
{ when he came in.

note: the imperfect tense is most often used for an action that was happening (going on) at a certain time. What is VITAL is to distinguish between the PRETÉRITO (past)

fui = I went

and the IMPERFECTO (imperfect), which is usually used with another verb in a sentence and which implies duration

comía mientras hablaba = I was eating while he was talking. The IMPERFECTO answers the question: What were you (in the midst of) doing when . . . ?

AR		ER – IR	
hablaba	I was speaking when . . .	vivía	I was living when . . .
hablabas	you were speaking . . .	vivías	you were living . . .
hablaba	he/she was speaking . . .	vivía	he/she was living . . .
	you were speaking . . .		you were living . . .
hablábamos	we were speaking . . .	vivíamos	we were living . . .
hablábais	you were speaking . . .	vivíais	you were living . . .
hablaban	they were speaking . . .	vivían	they were living . . .
	you were speaking . . .		you were living . . .

note: The above endings are added to the stem of the verb.

¿DORMÍAS CUANDO LLAMÉ?	Were you sleeping when I called?
Sí, dormía cuando llamaste.	Yes, I was sleeping when you called.
No, no dormía cuando llamaste.	No, I wasn't sleeping when you called.

¿HABLABAS MIENTRAS ESCRIBÍA?	Were you talking while he was writing?
Sí, hablaba mientras escribía.	Yes, I was talking while he was writing.
No, no hablaba mientras escribía.	No, I wasn't talking while he was writing.

VERBOS IRREGULARES (imperfecto)

SER	IR	VER
era	iba	veía
eras	ibas	veías
era	iba	veía
éramos	íbamos	veíamos
érais	íbais	veíais
eran	iban	veían

translate:

1) ¿Qué hacía Vd. ayer mientras yo dormía?
2) Comía cuando viniste.
3) Contestaba a la pregunta mientras los demás escuchaban.
4) Venía a vernos cuando sucedió el accidente.
5) Compraba un nuevo coche cuando encontré a este tío.
6) Los niños miraban la tele mientras sus padres comían.
7) Ganaba su vida mientras él dormía.
8) Bebíamos mientras trabajabas.
9) Cuando me llamaste, tomaba un baño.
10) Cuando entraste en la cocina, el gato tuvo miedo.
11) Hacíamos un viaje cuando cayó enferma.
12) Había mucha gente en casa cuando llegargon.
13) Mientras moría, su marido estaba con otra mujer.
14) Nací cuando mi padre estaba fuera del país.

translate:

1) What were you doing when I called?
2) Why were you people working when I was sleeping?
3) She was taking a test while I was watching television.
4) The maid was doing the housework when we came home.
5) I was driving when the accident happened.
6) She was getting married while her sister was getting divorced.
7) The students were making progress when the teacher had to leave them.
8) What were you doing while we were eating?
9) He was winning while I was losing.
10) Were you sleeping when I called?
11) Were they writing letters while we were playing?
12) While we were living in New York, we saw a lot of movies.
13) The plane was taking off when we saw it.
14) The father came home just when the kids were shouting.

insert the correct form (pretérito o imperfecto):

1) Pedro . . . (venir) cuando . . . (cenar).
2) . . . (escribir) una carta cuando . . . (llamar).
3) . . . (comer) mientras . . . (trabajar).
4) . . . (estar cansado) cuando . . . (llegar).
5) . . . (dejar de) leer cuando . . . (entrar).
6) . . . (leer) su última novela cuando . . . (llamar).
7) . . . (ver) al jefe cuando . . . (entrar) en la tienda.
8) . . . (hablar) cuando . . . (llegar).
9) . . . (andar) cuando . . . encontrar.
10) A las seis, . . . (volver) mientras . . . (trabajar).
11) Las secretarias . . . (hablar) cuando el jefe . . . (entrar) en el cuarto.
12) Cuando . . . (venir), . . . (comer).
13) Cuando . . . (salir), . . . (llover).
14) Cuando le . . . (ver), no le . . . (reconocer).
15) . . . (acabar) la clase cuando . . . (deber) salir.
16) . . . (soñar) mientras . . . (trabajar).
17) Cuando . . . (ver) a mi amigo, . . . (estar) en la calle.
18) . . . (estar triste) cuando te (encontrar) . . . ayer.
19) No . . . (saber) todavía cuando le . . . (ver).
20) . . . (estar decidiendo) cuando él . . . (decidir) para mí.
21) Cuando . . . (empezar) a trabajar, . . . (comenzar) a llover, y . . . (llover) durante dos horas.
22) . . . (estar hablando) cuando me . . . (hacer) una pregunta.
23) La poli . . . (llegar) cuando . . . (salir).
24) . . . (estar leyendo) los periódicos mientras su hijo . . . (mirar) la tele.
25) . . . (venir) a verme cuando . . . (comer).
26) . . . (preguntar) por qué le . . . (dar) este regalo.
27) ¿Por qué . . . (reir) cuando . . . (decir) eso?
28) . . . (estar durmiendo) cuando . . . (llamar).

VOCABULARIO

	traducción	sinónimo asociado	opuesto asociado
1. tiene suerte	you're lucky ≠ unlucky	es afortunado = por chiripa = luckily	desgraciado, desafortunado
2. hace poco tiempo	a little while ago, recently	no hace mucho, recientemente, últimamente	dentro de poco = in a little while; hace mucho = a long time ago.
3. ¿verdad?	right?	realmente = really	¡no es verdad! = you're kidding!
4. /(el) equipaje /hacer sus maletas	/baggage/to pack	preparar (la) maleta	deshacer la maleta = to unpack
5. (el) objetivo	aim	(el) fin, (el) blanco = target	
6. en un apuro	in a jam, a spot	en un atolladero = un lío	
7. estar orgulloso	to be proud ≠ ashamed	ufano	tener vergüenza
8. entusiasta	enthusiastic		indiferente = cool
9. (el) sueño	dream	(la) pesadilla = nightmare	
10. me preguntaba	I was wondering		
11. (la) firma	company, firm	(la) sociedad, (la) empresa, (la) compañía	
12. (el) paquete	package	(el) fardo, (el) bulto	
13. recuérdame . . .	remind me to . . .	acuérdame de . . .	
14. de primer orden	first rate ≠ second rate		de segundo orden; (la) pérdida de tiempo = waste of time
15. criticar	to criticise ≠ to praise	hablar mal de, hacer trizas = to (run) down someone	alabar
16. hacer progresos	to make progress	avanzar, mejorar = to improve	
17. derecho	straight ≠ crooked	recto	torcido
18. (la) muchedumbre	crowd	(el) mundo, (el) gentío, (la) gente	

100

LECCIÓN 21

CONDICIONAL (conditional) + sequence of tenses

Dice que **vendrá**.	She says she'll come.
Dijo que **vendría**.	She said she would come.

hablaría	
hablarías	
hablaría	would speak
hablaríamos	
hablaríais	
hablarían	

note: Add these endings to the infinitive of all verbs.

¿DIJO QUE HABLARÍA CON ÉL?	Did she say she would speak with him?
Sí, dijo que hablaría con él.	Yes, she said she would speak with him.
No, dijo que no hablaría con él.	No, she said she wouldn't speak with him.

compare:

Piensa que **puede** hacerlo.	He <u>feels</u> he <u>can</u> do it.
Pensó que **podría** hacerlo.	He <u>felt</u> he <u>could</u> do it.
Sé que **tiene** razón.	I <u>know</u> you're right.
Supe que **tendría** razón.	I <u>knew</u> you <u>would be</u> right.
Pienso que $\dfrac{\text{tengo}}{\text{debo}}$ que ir. ir.	I <u>think</u> I have to go.
Pensé que $\dfrac{\text{tendría}}{\text{debería}}$ que ir. ir.	I <u>thought</u> I <u>would</u> have to go.
Dice que **vendrá.**	She <u>says</u> she'll come.
Dijo que **vendría.**	She <u>said</u> she'd come.

VERBOS IRREGULARES (condicional)

VALER → **valdría**
to be worth

QUERER → **querría**
to want

HACER → **haría**
to make

SABER → **sabría**
to know

PONER → **pondría**
to put

PROPONER → **propondría**
to suggest

PODER → **podría**
to be able to

TENER → **tendría**
to have

HABER → **habría**
to have

CABER → **cabría**
to contain

DECIR → **diría**
to say

VENIR → **vendría**
to come

PREVENIR → **prevendría**
to warn

CONVENIR → **convendría**
to suit

SALIR → **saldría**
to go out

put the following sentences into the past:

1) Dice que hará sus maletas.
2) Pienso que tendrá miedo.
3) Sabemos que haremos progresos.
4) Saben que serán capaces de hacerlo.
5) Sabe que le buscará.
6) Le digo que saldré.
7) Escribe que vendrá la semana próxima.
8) Toma el tren que llegará a tiempo.
9) Pienso que estará harto pronto.
10) Mi madre sabe que conseguiré el divorcio.
11) ¿Piensas que se enfadará?
12) Te digo que no tendrás que venir.
13) Dice que hará muchas faltas porque no es bueno.
14) ¿Crees que tendrá miedo?

put the following sentences into the present:

1) No sabía que vendría.
2) Pensábamos que tomaríamos el tren esta mañana.
3) Supo que le gustaría tu novio.
4) Pensé que no estaría enfadada.
5) Decidí que iríamos al ciné.
6) Dijeron que no querían trabajar la semana próxima.
7) El jefe pensó que los negocios tendrían más éxito.
8) El escritor pensó que su libro sería el mejor del año.
9) Supimos que llegaríamos tarde.
10) Dijo que estaría muy malo.
11) Escribió que no vendría a la fiesta.
12) Soñé que iría a Africa.
13) Me pregunté si vendrían con nosotros.
14) Planéo que terminaría sus estudios este año.

103

translate and then put into the present:

1) He told me she would like to work part-time.
2) I knew that you would help us.
3) I thought my kids would bother you a lot.
4) I was convinced you would already be fed up.
5) She felt she looked ugly.
6) I knew you wouldn't be satisfied.
7) I thought that you would be right.
8) It seemed to us that it wouldn't be so important.
9) She said that she'd agree with you.
10) We thought that you'd be able to come.
11) It seemed that he would have to get a new job.
12) I didn't know that you would be so sick.
13) Didn't you know that I could help you?
14) Did you think I would be right?

translate and then put into the past:

1) She can't imagine that her husband's a bastard.
2) I know that you'll be lucky.
3) I want to know what you'll need.
4) She thinks she'll be able to go.
5) We don't understand what you're telling us.
6) Don't you see that I'll be fed up soon?
7) I'm convinced she'll need help.
8) I don't think he'll like the decision.
9) I know you won't be able to do it.
10) We feel she'll agree.
11) I think we'll have to leave now.
12) I feel I'll have to help her.
13) 1t happens that you don't know what you're saying.
14) She says she'll have to work hard.

104

VOCABULARIO

	traducción	sinónimo asociado	opuesto asociado
1. enfadado	angry ≠ satisfied	furioso; ponerse fuera de sí = to lose one's temper	
2. hacer planes	to plan to	planear; tener intención de = to intend to	
3. valiente	brave	valeroso	cobarde = coward
4. encontrar	/to find/to meet	hallar	buscar = to look for, perder = to lose
5. corriente	usual ≠ unusual	usual; típico = typical inhabitual	
6. ¡estoy harto!	I'm fed up!		
7. limpio	clean ≠ dirty	fragante, aseado, limpiar = to clean	sucio, ensuciar = to dirty
8. (el) cumpleaños	birthday	felicidades, felicitaciones = congratulations	
9. además	moreover, furthermore	más aún, además de = in addition to	
10. /¿otra cosa? /¿quién más? /¿qué más?	/something else? /who else? /what else?	alguien más = someone else; en otra parte = somewhere else	nada más = nothing else
11. tengo miedo	I'm afraid, frightened	estoy asustado, temeroso	
12. en cambio	on the other hand	por otro lado, por otra parte, aparte de = apart from; al contrario = on the contrary	
13. hacer trampas	to cheat	engañar	
14. según	according to		
15. tengo miedo que	I'm afraid that	me temo que	
16. (el) resultado	result	(la) conclusión, (la) salida	

LECCIÓN 22

SI = IF (conditional 2)

¿SI VD. TUV<u>IERA</u> DINERO, COMPRAR<u>Í</u>A UN COCHE?
    past subjunctive + conditional
If you <u>had</u> money, <u>would</u> you buy a car?

Sí, si tuv<u>ie</u>ra dinero, comprar<u>í</u>a un coche.
Yes, if I <u>had</u> money, I'<u>d</u> buy a car.

No, si tuv<u>ie</u>ra dinero, no comprar<u>í</u>a un coche.
No, if I <u>had</u> money, I <u>wouldn't</u> buy a car.

---

note: CAREFUL! This is complicated and tricky, as the tenses used in Spanish are not the same as in English!!

PAST SUBJUNCTIVE (two forms: RA, SE)

<u>AR</u>	<u>ER</u> – <u>IR</u>
Si habl<u>ara</u> . . .	Si com<u>iera</u> . . .
<u>se</u>	<u>se</u>
habl<u>aras</u>	com<u>ieras</u>
<u>ses</u>	<u>ses</u>
habl<u>ara</u>	com<u>iera</u>
<u>se</u>	<u>se</u>
habl<u>áramos</u>	com<u>iéramos</u>
<u>semos</u>	<u>semos</u>
habl<u>árais</u>	com<u>iérais</u>
<u>seis</u>	<u>seis</u>
habl<u>aran</u>	com<u>ieran</u>
<u>sen</u>	<u>sen</u>

---

note: — The 'se' endings are less used.
        — All these endings are added to the third-person plural stem of the verb in the past tense.

compare:

Si estoy enfermo, iré al médico.	If I'm sick, I'll go to the doctor.
Si estuviera enfermo, iría al médico.	If I were sick, I would go to the doctor.
Si puede ayudar, me lo dirá.	If she can help, she'll tell me.
Si pudiera ayudar, me lo diría.	If she could help, she'd tell me.
Si tienen tiempo vendrán.	If they have time, they'll come.
Si tuvieran tiempo, vendrían.	If they had time, they'd come.
Si tengo que hacerlo, estaré furioso.	If I have to do it, I'll be angry.
Si tuviera que hacerlo, estaría furioso.	If I had to do it, I'd be angry.

translate, and then put into the first IF (conditional) form:
e.g. ¿Si estuvieras enfermo, irías al médico?
  — If you were sick, would you go to the doctor?
  — ¿Si estás enfermo, irás al médico?

1) ¿Si tuvieras dinero, comprarías un piso nuevo?
2) ¿Si pudiera me ayudaría?
3) ¿Si viniera a verte, serías feliz?
4) Si los turistas tuvieran tiempo, irían a ver los museos.
5) Si la compañía tuviera éxito, el director estaría contento.
6) ¿Si no me entendiera, me lo diría?
7) Si lloviera, tomaríamos un paraguas.
8) Si tuviéramos que hacerlo, lo haríamos.
9) Si hiciera mal tiempo, no nos iríamos de paseo.
10) Si tuviéramos hambre, acabaríamos la carne de ayer.
11) ¿Si pudieras venir, vendrías solo?
12) Si te debiera dinero, te lo pagaría inmediatamente.
13) Si quisieras, te lo daría.
14) ¿Si estuviera en un apuro, me ayudarías?

answer in Spanish in the first and second form of IF (conditional):

1) If you're sick will you go to the doctor?
2) If I can't do it, will you help me?
3) If I don't have enough money, will you lend me some?
4) If the weather's nice, will they go to the beach?
5) If she has time, will she come with us?
6) If you go to Spain, will you meet interesting guys?
7) If I'm late, will you be angry?
8) If we work hard, will we earn a lot of money?
9) If you entertain tonight, will you invite me?
10) If it rains, will we go anyway?
11) If you feel better, will you have to go to the doctor?
12) If you're fed up, will you leave her?
13) If you catch a cold, will you sneeze a lot?
14) If his book fails, will he be disappointed?
15) If you lend me some dough, will I return it?
16) If you take a trip, can I come home with you?
17) If I have to go to the doctor, will you go with me?
18) If she doesn't know her pal's sick, will you tell her?
19) If we make a lot of progress, will we be happy?
20) If she loses the game, will she cry?
21) If her husband criticises her all the time, will she leave him?
22) If you can leave your husband, will you?
23) If the car's on sale, will you buy it?
24) If I want to stay, will you stay with me?
25) If the movie is crowded, will we go anyway?
26) If you work part-time, can you earn enough money?
27) If we try hard will we be successful?
28) If the novel is boring, will we read it anyway?
29) If they want to leave the kids with their mother-in-law, will she agree to take them?
30) If his girlfriend loves him, will he be happy?

VOCABULARIO

	traducción	sinónimo asociado	opuesto asociado
1. preferiría ir	I'd prefer going	me gustaría más = I'd rather	
2. (el) visitante	visitor	(el) invitado = guest	(el) huésped = host
3. /desilusionar/(la) desilusión	/to disappoint /disappointment	me ha desilusionado – he let me down	
4. ganar dinero	to earn money	ganarse la vida = to earn one's living	(el) desempleo = unemployment
5. ¡que se diviertan!	enjoy yourselves!	que lo pasen bien	nos divertimos mucho = we had a good time
6. exagerar	to exaggerate	pasarse de la raya = to go too far	
7. a partir de	as of	desde	
8. pasa que	it happens that	ocurre que	
9. desde entonces	ever since	desde aquellos días = aquellos tiempos = ever since, de ahora en adelante	hasta = until
10. proteger	to protect	amparar	desamparar
11. asegurarse	to make sure	afianzarse	
12. celebrar	to celebrate	dar una fiesta	
13. malo	naughty ≠ good	trasto, travieso	bueno
14. recibir	/to receive/entertain	tener compañía	enviar = mandar = to send
15. a veces	sometimes	algunas veces; de vez en cuando = from time to time	
16. más que	rather than		
17. ¡bienvenido!	welcome!	está como en su casa	
18. aullar	to yell, shout	gritar, chillar	cuchichear = whisper
19. pelearse	to fight	luchar, combatir = to struggle	

LECCIÓN 23

PRETÉRITO INDEFINIDO (indefinite past) = PRESENT PERFECT,
e.g. have spoken

he	I	**+ habl<u>ado</u>**
has	you	have spoken
ha	he, she, you, it	
hemos	we	**+ com<u>ido</u>**
habéis	you	have eaten
han	they, you	

note: — This corresponds to our present perfect for an indefinite past (you
don't know when).
— **haber** is an auxiliary verb only.
— To form the past participle you add 'ado' to the stem of the AR
verbs and 'ido' to the stem of the IR and ER verbs.

¿HAS TERMINADO EL LIBRO?	Have you finished the book?
Sí, he terminado el libro.	Yes, I have finished the book.
No, no he terminado el libro.	No, I have not finished the book.

note: You don't know 'when'.

```
┌─────────────────────────────────────────────────────────────────────┐
│ THERE ARE TWO PASTS IN SPANISH!!                                      │
│                                                                       │
│ PRESENT PERFECT              PAST                                     │
│ an action is finished, but you don't    an action is finished and the 'when' │
│ know 'when'                  is specified                            │
│                                                                       │
│ I HAVE EATEN in that restaurant.    I ATE in that restaurant LAST     │
│ (you don't know when)        WEEK.                                   │
│                                                                       │
│ HE COMIDO en este restaurante.    COMÍ en este restaurante LA         │
│                              SEMANA PASADA.                           │
└─────────────────────────────────────────────────────────────────────┘
```

DON'T GET SICK OVER THIS!!!! **MISTAKES ARE NOT IMPORTANT!!!!**
In general, the past is more often used than the present perfect.

translate:

1) Sí, he leído este libro. Lo leí en enero.
2) He escrito tres cartas hoy.
3) He ido a menudo a los Estados Unidos. Fui allí en mayo.
4) Mi marido ha visto esta película dos veces este mes.
5) Hemos comido mucho en este restaurante.
6) Fuimos allí el viernes pasado.
7) He comprado muchos vestidos recientemente.
8) Compré un abrigo ayer.
9) Ha estado a menudo embarazada.
10) Estuvo embarazada el año pasado.
11) Me ha ayudado mucho.
12) Me ayudó sobre todo el mes pasado.
13) He tenido que ver al médico a menudo recientemente.
14) Tuve que ver al médico la semana pasada.
15) Mi marido ha viajado a menudo.
16) Hizo un viaje a China el año pasado.

```
┌─────────────────────────────────────────────────────────────────┐
│  YA = ALREADY              NO TODAVÍA, NO AÚN = NOT               │
│                            YET                                    │
│  ¿HA LLEGADO YA?           Has he/she/you come already?           │
│  Sí, ya ha llegado.        Yes, he has already come.              │
│  No, no ha llegado  todavía.   No, he has not come yet.           │
│                     aún.                                          │
│  No, todavía no.           No, not yet.                           │
│    aún no.                                                        │
└─────────────────────────────────────────────────────────────────┘
```

translate:

1)   ¿Ha adivinado la respuesta ya?
2)   ¿Ha pegado ya a su mujer?
3)   Mi marido no me ha llamado todavía.
4)   ¿Ha venido el jefe ya? No, todavía no.
5)   ¿Has ido alguna vez a España? Sí dos veces ya.
6)   ¿Has encontrado a un tío interesante ya? No, todavía no.

translate and give the affirmative and negative answers:

e.g. Has she called you yet?
        — Sí, ya me ha llamado.
        — No, no me ha llamado todavía.

1)   Have we already made progress in Spanish?
2)   Have we earned a lot of money yet?
3)   Are you fed up already?
4)   Have you met an interesting gal yet?
5)   Have they visited their mother-in-law yet?
6)   Has she stopped working already?
7)   Has he already sold his car?
8)   Have you had breakfast yet?
9)   Has she taken her bath already?
10) Have you caught a cold this winter yet?
11) Have you people eaten yet?
12) Have you learned another language already?
13) Have you found your purse yet?
14) Has he packed already?

112

Insert either the pretérito indefinido (past indefinite) or préterito (past):

1) . . . (ver) la película la semana pasada.
2) ¿ . . . (ver) esta película?
3) ¿ . . . (ir) alguna vez a Nueva York?
4) . . . (tomar) el avión para Madrid la semana pasada.
5) . . . (fumar) demasiado anoche.
6) ¿Le . . . (hablar) hoy?
7) . . . (hablar) con él hace unos días.
8) Piensa que ya . . . (casarse) dos veces.
9) . . . (ver) esa película dos veces.
10) La . . . (ver) por primera vez el año pasado.
11) . . . (empezar) a estudiar español hace un mes.
12) . . . (aprender) mucho en esta clase.
13) No . . . (ver) a su abuela todavía.
14) . . . (ir) a Italia muchas veces.
15) Te . . . (llamar) dos veces hoy.
16) La última vez . . . (ser) hace una hora.
17) Su amigo . . . (venir) hace poco y . . . (salir) juntos hace cinco minutos.
18) . . . (preguntar) muchas cosas al profesor en esta clase.
19) . . . (hacer) frío ayer.
20) . . . (llover) a menudo este invierno.
21) Mi hermano . . . (vivir) en Nueva York el año pasado. . . . (vivir) en varios estados en los Estados Unidos.
22) . . . (comprar) esta casa en 1975 y . . . (vivir) allí durante cinco años.
23) Antes de venir a Francia, . . . (trabajar) como secretaria.
24) También . . . (trabajar) en muchos otros trabajos.
25) . . . (necesitar) ayuda la semana pasada pero esta semana todavía no . . (necesitar) ninguna.
26) . . . (dar) un regalo para mi cumpleaños.
27) . . . (trabajar) aquí durante diez años.
28) Le . . . (ver) muchas veces desde su accidente. En efecto le . . . (ver) ayer.

MISTAKES ARE NOT IMPORTANT!!!!!!

VERBOS IRREGULARES (pretérito perfecto)

PRIMER GRUPO: AR

dar (to give)	→ dado	pensar (to think)	→ pensado
estar (to be)	→ estado	contar (to count)	→ contado
andar (to walk)	→ andado	acordar (to remember)	→ acordado
empezar (to begin)	→ empezado	jugar (to play)	→ jugado
sentar(se) (to sit)	→ sentado	rogar (to beg)	→ rogado
cerrar (to shut)	→ cerrado	fijar (to fix)	→ fijado
despertar (to wake up)	→ despertado		

SEGUNDO GRUPO: ER

valer (to be worth)	→ valido	volver (to become)	→ vuelto
ver (to see)	→ visto	oler (to smell)	→ olido
querer (to want)	→ querido	mover (to move)	→ movido
hacer (to make)	→ hecho	entender (to understand)	→ entendido
traer (to bring)	→ traido	conocer (to know)	→ conocido
caer (to fall)	→ caido	reconocer (to recognize)	→ reconocido
saber (to know)	→ sabido	parecer (to seem)	→ parecido
poner (to put)	→ puesto	pertenecer (to belong)	→ pertenecido
proponer (to suggest)	→ propuesto	convencer (to convince)	→ convencido
poder (can)	→ podido	establecer (to set up)	→ establecido
ser (to be)	→ sido	nacer (to be born)	→ nacido
tener (to have)	→ tenido	proteger (to protect)	→ protegido
haber (to have)	→ habido	leer (to read)	→ leído
caber (to contain)	→ cabido	llover (to rain)	→ llovido
soler (to be used)	→ solido	coger (to take)	→ cogido
romper (to break)	→ roto	doler (to hurt)	→ dolido

TERCER GRUPO: IR

oír (to hear)	→ oído	pedir (to ask)	→ pedido
decir (to say)	→ dicho	conseguir (to reach)	→ conseguido
venir (to come)	→ venido	vestir (to dress)	→ vestido
prevenir (to warn)	→ prevenido	reñir (to quarrel)	→ reñido
convenir (to suit)	→ convenido	concluir (to conclude)	→ concluido
salir (to go out)	→ salido	huir (to escape)	→ huido
dormir (to sleep)	→ dormido	construir (to build)	→ construido
morir (to die)	→ muerto	conducir (to drive)	→ conducido
sentir (to feel)	→ sentido	distinguir (to distinguish)	→ distinguido
preferir (to prefer)	→ preferido	elegir (to choose)	→ elegido
divertir (to enjoy)	→ divertido	reír (to laugh)	→ reído
repetir (to repeat)	→ repetido	desvestir (to undress)	→ desvestido
seguir (to follow)	→ seguido	servir (to serve)	→ servido
abrir (to open)	→ abierto		
escribir (to write)	→ escrito		
cubrir (to cover)	→ cubierto		
freir (to fry)	→ frito		

VOCABULARIO

	traducción	sinónimo asociado	opuesto asociado
1. golpear	to hit, beat	pegar, dar una azotaina = una paliza = to spank	
2. mentir	to lie ≠ to tell the truth	(la) mentira = lie	decir la verdad
3. parecer	to look, seem	me parece que . . . = it looks like . . . ; parece bien = it sounds good	
4. ya que	since, as	dado que, puesto que, después de que	
5. ¡qué follón!	what a mess!	¡qué jaleo!	
6. el norte	north	(el) sur, este, oeste	
7. echo de menos a mi familia/mi familia me echa de menos	/I miss my family /my family misses me	extraño a mi familia	
8. ¡vamos!	/let's go/come on now	¡anda!	
9. embarazada	pregnant	en estado de buena esperanza	(el) aborto = abortion, miscarriage
10. tímido	shy ≠ brazen	vergonzoso	es un fresco
11. /Francia/los Estados Unidos /Italia/China	/France/United States/Italy/China	franceses, americanos, italianos, chinos	
12. ya	already ≠ not yet		no aún, no todavía
13. /Alemania /España /Inglaterra	/Germany/Spain /England	alemanes, españoles, ingleses	
14. ¡qué lío!	what a fuss!	armar un lío = to make a fuss	
15. adivinar	to guess	acertar	

LECCIÓN 24

VOY A	=	I'M GOING TO
Voy a ir mañana.		I'm going to go tomorrow.
Va a verle hoy.		He/she's going to see him/her/you today.

ACABAR DE + INFINITIVE	=	TO HAVE JUST . . .
Acaba de salir.		He has just left.
A acabamos de hacerlo.		We've just done it.

TODAVÍA = STILL	≠ **YA NO** = **NO MÁS** = NO MORE
¿Está enfermo todavía?	Is he still sick?
Sí, está enfermo todavía.	Yes, he's still sick.
No, no está más enfermo.	No, he isn't sick any more.
No, ya no.	No, no more.

¿ ... ... GUSTA?	=	DO YOU LIKE?
¿Le gusta el café (a Vd.)?		Do you like coffee?
Sí, me gusta.		Yes, I like coffee.
No, no me gusta.		No, I don't like coffee.

note: — Do they like books? = ¿Les gustan los libros?
      — Do they like coffee? = ¿Les gusta el café?
      — Do you like them?   = ¿Te gustan (a tí)?
                      = ¿Le gustan (a Vd.)?

UN POCO DE	=	A LITTLE
¿Tiene un poco de dinero?		Have you a little money?
Sí, tengo un poco.		Yes, I have a little.
No, no tengo nada.		No, I haven't any.

SE	=	ONE, YOU, etc.
Se habla inglés aquí.		English is spoken here.
Se bebe mucho vino en España.		One (you) drink(s) a lot of wine in Spain.

117

translate:

1) Acaba de salir ahora.
2) ¿Están todavía en huelga? No, ya no.
3) Se quieren todavía y nosotros también.
4) ¿Le gusta el café? No, no me gusta.
5) ¿Tienes un poco de dinero? Sí tengo un poco.
6) Sólo se habla español aquí.
7) ¿Te duele todavía? No, no me duele más.
8) ¿Les gusta el pollo?
9) Acabamos de terminar este trabajo.
10) Voy a terminar otro.
11) ¿Están casados todavía? No, ya no.
12) ¿Te molesta todavía? Sí, me molesta todavía.
13) ¿Trabajan todavía media jornada? No, ya no.
14) ¿Piensas que está enfermo todavía?

translate:

1) Are they still married? No, not any more.
2) Do you (does anyone) speak English here?
3) Do you have some sugar? No, I don't have any.
4) Do you like vegetables? Yes, I like them.
5) Do they still argue a lot? No, not any longer.
6) Are you going to go with her this evening?
7) He left just a few minutes ago.
8) Are you still tired? No, I'm not tired any more.
9) Do they like fish? No, they don't like it.
10) Do you know how to drive?
11) I'm going to go on strike.
12) They have just gone out.
13) Do you still like to earn a lot of money? Yes, I still like to earn a lot of money.
14) One eats a lot of fish in Spain.

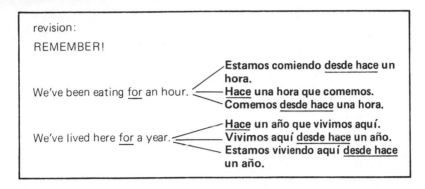

revision:

REMEMBER!

We've been eating <u>for</u> an hour.
- Estamos comiendo <u>desde hace</u> un hora.
- <u>Hace</u> una hora que comemos.
- Comemos <u>desde hace</u> una hora.

We've lived here <u>for</u> a year.
- <u>Hace</u> un año que vivimos aquí.
- Vivimos aquí <u>desde hace</u> un año.
- Estamos viviendo aquí <u>desde hace</u> un año.

translate in the three possible forms:

e.g. I've been listening to you for an hour.
- Hace una hora que le escucho.
- Le escucho desde hace una hora.
- Estoy escuchándole desde hace una hora.

1) I've been watching TV for an hour.
2) They've been living in Madrid for five years.
3) The kids have been playing for two hours.
4) He's been working in this company for twelve years.
5) She's been sleeping for ten hours.
6) We've been taking Spanish lessons for two years.
7) We've been eating for an hour.
8) They've been quarrelling for half an hour.
9) You've been annoying me for too long.
10) I've been walking for an hour.
11) You've been teaching us Spanish for many months.
12) We've been drinking a lot since our marriage.
13) You've been lying to me since yesterday.
14) I've been looking for my bag for hours.
15) She's been criticizing me since the beginning.
16) I've been paying too much since the beginning.
17) He's been taking a trip since January.
18) The kids have been crying since this morning.

1.	— a eso de (la una)	— about (one)	14.	de aquí a . . . (invierno)	by winter
	— más o menos	— more or less	15.	desde el principio	from the first
2.	— ¿cuándo?	— when?			
	— ¿desde cuándo?	— since when?	16.	— de veras	— really
				— de verdad	
	— ¿hasta cuándo?	— till when?, how long?		— sin interrupción	— permanently
3.	en efecto	indeed	17.	todo el día	all day long
4.	todavía siempre	still	18.	afortunada- mente	fortunately
5.	uno de cada diez	one out of ten	19.	— por todas partes	— all over
6.	por falta	by mistake		— en cualquier parte	— anywhere
7.	a menos de que	unless		— sitio	
8.	— además	— furthermore	20.	— en alguna parte	— somewhere
	— más aún	— in addition to		— en ninguna parte	— nowhere
9.	sin embargo	all the same			
10.	— hace poco	— a little while ago	21.	— como siempre	as usual
	— no hace mucho			— como de costumbre	
	— dentro de poco	— in a little while	22.	en este caso	if so
11.	durante un momento	for a while	23.	para decirlo así	so to speak
12.	de lejos	by far	24.	aún cuando	even if
13.	— en efecto	— in fact	25.	por con- siguiente	consequently
	— en realidad	— as a matter of fact	26.	la semana que viene	this coming week

120

VOCABULARIO

	traducción	sinónimo asociado	opuesto asociado
1. media jornada	part-time ≠ full-time		jornada completa
2. (el) sindicato	union	ponerse en huelga = to go on strike	
3. conocido	famous		desconocido
4. quejarse	to complain ≠ to be satisfied	gruñir = to kick, (grumble)	estar satisfecho
5. (la) razón	reason, explanation	(la) explicación, (el) detalle = detail, (el) hecho = fact, (el) dato	
6. (la) idea	idea	(el) pensamiento = thought	
7. ite das cuenta!	do you realize!	just think! = ifíjate!	no me dí cuenta = I didn't realize
8. (el) accidente	accident	(la) catástrofe, (el) desastre	
9. molestar	to annoy, bother	fastidiar, dar lata	
10. es una lata	it's/he's a pain in the neck!, nuisance	(la) pelma, (el) latoso, (el) pesado	
11. reñir	to argue	regañar = to quarrel	llevarse bien = to get on well
12. (la) riña	argument	disputa	
13. tener mucha cara	to have guts	(la) caradura = (el) rostro = nerve	
14. principal	main, leading	mayor = importante = important	
15. por lo visto	evidently, apparently	evidentemente, al parecer, por supuesto = naturally	indefinido = impreciso = vague
16. persuadir	to persuade	convencer = to convince	
17. no sé conducir	I don't <u>know how</u> to drive		
18. en caso de que	in case	por si acaso, por si	

LECCIÓN 25

LO QUE =	WHAT
¿Es lo que quiere?	Is that <u>what</u> you want?
Sí, es lo que quiero.	Yes, this is <u>what</u> I want.
No, no es lo que quiero.	No, it isn't <u>what</u> I want.

note: Todo lo que = all that.

Sé lo que piensa	I know <u>what</u> he thinks.
Sé que . . .	I know <u>that</u> . . .
Lo que sé es que viene.	<u>What</u> I know is that he's coming.
Sé que viene.	I know (<u>that</u>) he's coming.
Es lo que quiero decir.	That's <u>what</u> I mean.
Sé lo que quiere decir.	I know <u>what</u> he means.
Lo que quiero decir es . . .	<u>What</u> I mean is . . .

translate:

1) No es lo que piensas.
2) No es lo que quiero decir.
3) No entiendo lo que Vd. quiere.
4) Sé lo que te han dicho.
5) No sé que decir.
6) Lo que me hace falta es mucho dinero.

translate:

1) Do you know what she wants to eat?
2) We know what we have to do.
3) That's what worries me.
4) Do you know what he thinks?
5) What interests me is to be able to go now.
6) That's what she means.
7) What I know is you're wrong.
8) I think that is what he wants.
9) What she needs is a nice boyfriend.
10) I can't do what you want me to.
11) He won't know what to do.
12) What he has to do is to finish the work immediately.

−ING (present participle)	=	INFINITIVO (infinitive)
sin pagar		with<u>out</u> paying
después de comer		<u>after</u> eating having eaten
<u>antes</u> de ir		<u>before</u> going
en <u>vez</u> de comer		<u>instead</u> of eating
<u>al</u> entrar		<u>upon</u> (<u>while</u>) entering

ESTAR ACOSTUMBRADO A = SOLER = TO BE USED TO

Estas acostumbrado a comer mucho? **Sueles comer mucho?**	Are you used to eating a lot?
Sí, estoy acostumbrado a comer mucho. **Sí, suelo comer mucho.**	Yes, I'm used to eating a lot.

HACER FALTA	=	TO NEED
¿<u>Te hace falta</u> **ayuda?** **¿<u>Necesitas</u>**		Do you need help?
Sí, <u>me hace falta</u> **ayuda.** **Sí <u>necesito</u>**		Yes, I need help.
No, no <u>me hace falta</u> **ayuda.** **No, no <u>necesito</u>**		No, I don't need help.

123

CUYO	= WHOSE, OF WHICH
La mujer cuyo marido está muerto.	The woman <u>whose</u> husband is dead.
El hombre cuya casa es grande.	The man <u>whose</u> house is big.
Los niños cuyos perros están malos.	The children <u>whose</u> dogs are sick.
Las casas cuyas puertas son blancas.	The houses <u>whose</u> doors are white.

note: 'cuyo' must precede the noun it modifies and agree in number and gender with it.

translate:

1) ¿Has notado que le hace falta más dinero?
2) Salió sin pagar.
3) El hombre cuya mujer ha muerto hace poco es mi hermano.
4) No suelo beber mucho por la tarde.
5) El escritor cuya novela tenía éxito está aquí.
6) En vez de hablar, vamos a hacer algo.
7) Los niños cuyos juguetes están en el suelo son míos.
8) Quiero comerlo antes y no después de ir.
9) La policía no está acostumbrada a matar a los bandidos.
10) Te hacen falta los periódicos de hoy.

translate:

1) The gangsters left without stealing anything.
2) The underworld is used to taking drugs.
3) The woman whose husband died last week is famous.
4) Instead of eating now, do you want to go and see her at the hospital?
5) Do you need some money?
6) The kids whose parents are divorced are often more successful later.
7) Upon entering I saw him talking with the other broad.
8) We're not used to dying before our parents.
9) The journalist whose book was a failure is a friend of mine.
10) Without saying anything, she hit him.
11) Do you mind if I'm not used to that kind of answer?
12) Instead of arguing explain to me what you want.

ADVERBIOS Y FRASES 5

1. **sin que**	without	15. **— en breve**	to make a long
2. **— ahora**	— at present	**— total**	story short
— para el	— for the time	**— en resumén**	
momento	being	16. **si fuera solo**	if only
— de momento		17. **como es así**	in the circum-
3. **de una forma**	somehow		stances
y otra		18. **— seguramente**	— surely
4. **— se lo ruego**	— by all means	**— seguro**	— definitely
— por todos	— by any means	19. **— permanenta-**	for good
los medios		**mente**	
5. **en cierto modo**	in a way	**— para siempre**	
6. **después de**	after all	20. **completamente**	altogether
todo		21. **— el colmo**	on top of
7. **cada vez más**	more and more	**— por encima**	
8. **de aquí a**	within a week	22. **— finalemente**	— all in all
9. **antes que**	before	**— pensándolo**	— after all
10. **dentro de una**	a week from	**bien**	
semana	today	**— en fin**	
11. **poco tiempo**	shortly before	23. **en este caso**	in that case
12. **a parte de**	apart from	24. **con tal que**	as long as
13. **trás**	behind	25. **a lo mejor**	at best
14. **cualquiera que**	regardless	26. **hasta ahora**	up to now
sea		27. **— poco importa**	— no matter
		— no importa	— no matter
			whatever
		28. **por eso**	that's why

VOCABULARIO

	traducción	sinónimo asociado	opuesto asociado
1. (el) fuego	fire	(el) bombero = fire-man	
2. (el) gangster	gangster	(el) bandido, (el) ladrón = robber; (el) estafador = crook; (el) gambero = hood	
3. robar	to steal	hurtar, afanar	
4. (la) prisión	jail	(la) cárcel	
5. detener	to arrest ≠ release	coger, pescar = atrapar = to nab	soltar
6. (el) robo	burglary	(el) hold-up, (el) atraco	
7. /matar/(el) ase-sino/(el) asesinato	/to kill/the murderer/the murder	(el) homicida = killer	
8. tirar	/to shoot/to throw	disparar, (el) revólver = gun; (la) bala = bullet	coger = to catch
9. honrado	honest	recto = straight	deshonesto = crooked
10. (la) cochinada	dirty trick	(la) mala jugada; (la) cerdada = low deal	
11. (el) soborno	bribe		
12. (el) periodista	journalist	(el) reportero	
13. (el) candidato	candidate	votar = to vote	
14. circunstancias	circumstances		
15. (la) droga	drugs		
16. escaparse	to escape	huir = to get away	
17. liar	to hustle	engañar = to con; pegársela a unos = to take someone in; embarullar	
18. (el) hampa	underworld		
19. su política es . . .	his policy is		
20. (la) trampa	trick	(la) emboscada = trap	

VOCABULARIO

	traducción	sinónimo asociado	opuesta asociado
1. (la) ventaja	advantage ≠ disadvantage	aprovechar = to take advantage of	(el) inconveniente
2. demasiado bien	only too well		
3. no puedo pasarme sin	can't help + ing	no podía pasarme sin = I couldn't help	
4. casi	almost + verb	casi me caí = I almost fell	
5. ¡bueno, bueno!	come now!	oye, cuéntalo a otro = I don't buy it	
6. (la) fuerza	strength ≠ weakness	(el) punto fuerte = strong point	(el) punto débil = weak point
7. ¿le molesta . . . ?	do you mind . . . ?	¿le importa . . . ?	no me molesta = I don't mind
8. tardé una hora	it took me an hour	me llevó una hora	
9. rápido	fast ≠ slow	veloz, pronto	lento, despacio
10. despierto	awake ≠ asleep	despejado	adormecido
11. /(la) vida /vivo	/life/alive	viviente = living	(la) muerte = death, muerto = dead
12. morir	to die ≠ to be born		nacer
13. (la) tontería	nonsense	burradas, tonto = bobo = distraído = silly	
14. notar	to notice	observar, mencionar = to mention	
15. (el) periódico	newspaper	(la) revista = magazine	
16. /proponer/(la) propuesta	/to suggest /suggestion	aconsejar = to advise, (el) consejo = a piece of advice	
17. es culpa mía	it's my fault		
18. como si	as if		

127

LECCIÓN 26

HELP!!

SI = IF (conditional 3)

first form

Si tengo dinero, compraré un coche.
If I have the money, I'll buy a car.

second form

Si tuviera dinero, compraría un coche.
If I had the money, I would buy a car.

third form

SI HUBIERA TENIDO DINERO, HUBIERA COMPRADO UN COCHE.
IF I HAD HAD THE MONEY I WOULD HAVE BOUGHT A CAR.

note: This is extremely complex — **the killer!!**

PAST PERFECT SUBJUNCTIVE = PAST SUBJUNCTIVE OF **HABER**
(RA or SE) + PAST PARTICIPLE

Si hubiera	**hubiera**	
se		
hubieras	**hubieras**	
ses		
hubiera tenido	**hubiera** comprado	
se		
hubiéramos	**hubiéramos**	
hubiérais	**hubiérais**	
hubieran	**hubieran**	

note: Remember the 'se' endings are less often used.

¿SI HUBIERAS TENIDO DINERO HUBIERAS COMPRADO UN COCHE?
If you had had the money, would you have bought a car?

Sí, si hubiera tenido dinero, hubiera comprado un coche.
No, si no hubiera tenido dinero, no hubiera comprado un coche.

¿SI HUBIERAS ESTADO ENFERMO, HUBIERAS IDO A LA CAMA?
If you had been sick, would you have gone to bed?

Sí, si hubiera estado enfermo, hubiera ido a la cama.
No, si no hubiera estado enfermo, no hubiera ido a la cama.

SI VOY, IRÁS TAMBIÉN.
If I go, you'll go too.

SI FUERA, IRÍAS TAMBIÉN.
If I went, you'd go too.

SI HUBIERA IDO, HUBIERAS IDO TAMBIÉN.
If I had gone, you would have gone too.

SI ES NECESARIO HACERLO, LO HARÉ.
If I have to do it, I'll do it.

SI FUERA NECESARIO HACERLO, LO HARÍA.
If I had to do it, I'd do it.

SI HUBIERA SIDO NECESARIO, LO HUBIERA HECHO.
If I had had to do it, I would have done it.

SI PUEDO, VENDRÉ.
If I can I'll come.

SI PUDIERA, VENDRÍA.
If I could, I'd come.

SI HUBIERA PODIDO, HUBIERA VENIDO.
If I could have, I would have come.

SI ESTOY ENFERMO, IRÉ A VER AL MÉDICO.
If I'm sick, I'll go to the doctor.

SI ESTUVIERA ENFERMO, IRÍA A VER AL MÉDICO.
If I were sick, I'd go to the doctor.

SI HUBIERA ESTADO ENFERMO, HUBIERA IDO A VER AL MÉDICO.
If I had been sick, I would have gone to the doctor.

SI SOY RICO, COMPRARÉ UN COCHE.
If I'm rich, I'll buy a car.

SI FUESE RICO, COMPRARÍA UN COCHE.
If I were rich, I'd buy a car.

SI HUBIERA, SIDO RICO, HUBIERA COMPRADO UN COCHE.
If I had been rich, I would have bought a car.

translate, then give the second and third forms of IF:
e.g. If Jane comes, she will help me.
— Si Juanita viniera, me ayudaría.
— Si Juanita hubiera venido, me hubiera ayudado.

1) Si tiene éxito, tendrá muchas mujeres.
2) Si puedes venir, estaré feliz.
3) Si le dan un soborno, el jefe estará feliz.
4) Si hay que hacerlo, te ayudaré.
5) Si llueve, no iremos.
6) Si no me prestas dinero, no podré comprar un coche.
7) Si no tengo que trabajar, jugaré con mi gato.
8) Si puedo elegir, tomaré éste.
9) Si tengo tiempo, encontraré un trabajo mejor.
10) Si sé que estás enfermo, vendré con sopa.
11) Si te parece mejor, haré como dices.
12) Si el escritor es rico, no trabaja más.
13) Si hay que hablarle, lo haré yo.
14) ¿Si puede venir, vendrás con él?
15) ¿Si no sabe que su hermana está embarazada, se lo dirás?
16) Si me desilusionas, estaré infeliz.
17) Si no tiene intención de hacerlo, no te pedirá tu opinión.
18) Si no haces tus deberes, el profesor te dejará.
19) Si no entiendes te explicaré.
20) Si tienes suerte estaré contenta por tí.
21) Si te hace daño, no seguiré haciéndolo.
22) Si el zoo está abierto, iremos a ver los monos.
23) Si necesitas frutas, sé donde puedes comprarlas.
24) Si algo va al revés moriré.
25) Si quieres, podremos aprovechar el buen tiempo.
26) Si robas, con mucha suerte no irás a la cárcel.
27) Si le haces una cochinada, la policía te detendrá.
28) Si no adelgazas, tu marido te dejará.

translate into the three Spanish conditional forms:

e.g. If I'm sick, I'll go to the doctor.
- Si estoy enfermo, iré al médico.
- Si estuviera enfermo, iría al médico.
- Si hubiera estado enfermo, hubiera ido al médico.

1) If you wind up the work today, we'll go shopping.
2) If the film is no great shakes, I won't go.
3) If the writer is crummy, they won't read his books.
4) If you lose weight your husband will be happy.
5) If he dies, I'll be sad.
6) If I have to go, will you come with me?
7) If he can help you, I know he will.
8) If the cops catch the killer, he'll go to prison.
9) If the politician is honest, we'll be surprised.
10) If the reporter has to give a bribe, he'll give a big one.
11) If the gangster steals a lot of dough, he'll find a politician to protect him.
12) If everything goes wrong, I'll go to bed.
13) If she can't come she'll call.
14) If they have to pay the bill again, they'll be furious.
15) If you lie again, I'll be fed up.
16) If you can guess, it will be amazing.
17) If she's pregnant it won't be by her husband.
18) If you continue to yell, I'll hang up.
19) If you disappoint me again, I'll have to leave you.
20) If he earns a lot of money, I'll marry him.
21) If you decide now, you can come with us.
22) If you plan to go, you must tell me.
23) If you want to get your plane, you must pack now.
24) If you have a headache, you can rest.
25) If the murder happens at his house, will he be worried?
26) If we can't call him, will he understand?
27) If we can win, will we have a lot of money?
28) If the kids don't want to, will they go to the zoo anyhow?

132

VOCABULARIO

	traducción	sinónimo asociado	opuesto asociado
1. completar	to complete, finish	acabar, terminar, finalizar = to wind up	emprender = to undertake
2. (la) condición	condition	(la) posición, (el) estado = state	
3. ir al revés	to go wrong	salir mal; empeorar = to get worse	ir mejor = to go better
4. /(el) fruto/(la) manzana/(el) melocotón/(la) naranja	/fruit/apple/peach /orange	grapefruit = (el) pomelo; (el) limón = lemon; (el) plátano = banana	
5. (la) barba	beard	afeitarse = to shave	
6. /(el) cuadro/(el) artista	/picture/artist	pintar = to paint, (la) pintura = painting, (el) pintor = painter	
7. (el) escritor	writer	(la) novela = novel	
8. /(la) silueta /(el) régimen	/figure/diet	(la) dieta, (la) línea	
9. (el) cuerpo	body	(el) cuello = neck; (la) espalda = shoulder	
10. demasiado delgado	underweight ≠ overweight	flaco = slim	demasiado gordo = pesado = heavy
11. adelgazar	to lose weight	bajar de peso	engordar = to gain weight
12. /(el) salón de peluquería /marcar el pelo	beauty parlour /shampoo (US wash) and set	(el) pelo = hair; (el) barbero = barber	
13. /(el) zoo/(el) animal/(el) animal doméstico	/zoo/animal/pet	(el) tigre = tiger; (el) león = lion; (el) elefante = elephant; (el) ave = (el) pájaro = bird; (el) mono = monkey; (el) oso = bear; (el) pato = duck; (la) vaca = cow; (el) caballo = horse; (la) oveja = sheep	
14. anterior	previous, former	precedente	posterior, el último = the latter

LECCIÓN 27

TENER QUE — **HAY QUE** — **DEBER** = TO HAVE TO, MUST
  present   past

I must/have to go   I had to go

debo   debía
tengo que } ir   tenía/tuve que }   ir
hay que   }   había que   }

es menester)   era menester)
  necesario } ir   necesario } ir
  preciso   )   preciso   )

¿TIENE QUE IR AHORA?   Must you go now?

Sí, tengo que ir ahora.   Yes, I must go now.
No, no tengo que ir ahora.   No, I don't have to go now.

¿TUVE QUE IR AYER?   Did you have to go yesterday?

Sí, tuve que ir ayer.   Yes, I had to go yesterday.
No, no tuve que ir ayer.   No, I didn't have to go yesterday.

DEBERÍA	=	SHOULD
¿Debería decirle?		Should I tell her?
Sí, debería decirle.		Yes, you should tell her.
No, no debería decirle.		No, you shouldn't tell her.

DEBERÍA HABER + participle	=	SHOULD HAVE
¿Debería haberle dicho.		Should I have told her?
Sí, debería haberle dicho.		Yes, you should have told her.
No, no debería haberle dicho.		No, you shouldn't have told her.

note: hubiera debido decirle = alternative form (more formal).

DEBE + infinitive	=	MUST BE
No está aquí, debe estar enfermo.		He isn't here, he must be sick.
No estaba aquí, debe haber estado enfermo.		He wasn't here, he must have been sick.

translate:

1) Debería haber trabajado más rápido.
2) Ya no está enferma. Debe ser un buen médico.
3) Debería haberlo dicho antes.
4) No tengo que ir ahora.
5) Es preciso ir mañana.
6) No deberías haberle hablado así.
7) El abrigo es barato. Deben haber bajado los precios.
8) Es menester tomar el avión para ir a Madrid.
9) No puedo encontrar mi paragüas. Debo haberlo perdido.
10) Hay que llamarla de todas maneras.
11) Debería comer en vez de hablar tanto.
12) Debo echar la carta, ahora mismo.
13) ¿Tenías que retirarte el año pasado?
14) No contestó. No debe haberle entendido.

translate:

1) I'm supposed to go this evening.
2) Do we have to pay a lot of dough for the house?
3) Should a killer go to jail?
4) I should call her tonight but I won't.
5) Do you have to work this weekend?
6) Why did they do that? They must be crazy.
7) I must speak to you.
8) Should he buy her a gift for her birthday?
9) The men didn't come. The unions must be on strike.
10) The boss isn't here. He must be sick.
11) We don't have to work tonight.
12) In my opinion you should accept what he is doing.
13) I have to admit you're right.
14) He shouldn't beat his wife.

VOCABULARIO

	traducción	sinónimo asociado	opuesto asociado
1. sería mejor que + verb	you'd better + verb	harías mejor en	
2. /(la) oficina de correos/(el) sello	/post office/stamp	(la) carta = letter, por avión = by air mail	
3. /(el) correo /echar al correo	/mail/to mail	(los) correos = post office	
4. cabezón	stubborn	testarudo, terco	
5. mudarse	to move	instalarse = to move in	
6. /(la) tierra /(el) mundo	/earth, land /world	(la) propiedad = property; (el) universo = universe	
7. /(la) corrida/(el) toro/(el) torero	/bullfight/bull /bullfighter	(el) ruedo = arena	
8. ¡qué bonita es!	how pretty she is!		
9. /(la) montaña /(el) lago/(el) campo	/mountain/lake /country	(el) río = river	
10. /(el) sobre/(la) postal	envelope, post card	(la) firma = signature	
11. aceptar	to accept ≠ to refuse	admitir = to admit	rehusar = negar = to deny
12. a mi parecer	in my opinion	en cuanto a = para mí = as for me	
13. arreglado	settled	solucionado = set	desarreglado
14. (la) situación	situation	(la) función = function	
15. (el) camión	lorry (US truck)	(la) furgoneta = van	
16. (la) parte	part ≠ whole	(la) mitad = half; (la) porción, (el) trozo = piece	
17. retirarse	to retire	dimitir = to resign; (la) dimisión = resignation	
18. describir	to describe	pintar = to depict	
19. permitir	allow ≠ forbid	dejar = to let	prohibir, impedir

LECCIÓN 28

TAN QUE = SO (adjective, adverb)

Está tan enfermo que no puede trabajar.
He's so sick that he can't work.

TANTO! (verbs, nouns) = SO MUCH, SO MANY

¡Tiene tanto dinero!   He has so much money!
¡Habla tanto!   He talks so much!

MUCHO, MUY   = VERY

MUCHO   **MUY**
(verbs, nouns)   (adjectives, adverbs)

Tiene mucho dinero.   **Es muy rico.**
¿Tiene mucho?   **Trabaja muy lentamente.**

---

translate:

1) Su novio es tan gracioso que nunca es aburrido.
2) El jefe estaba tan enfadado que salió.
3) ¡Hablas tanto!
4) Come tanto que engorda mucho.
5) Está tan cansada que va a quedarse en cama.
6) ¡Hemos bailado tanto!

translate:

1) She is so stubborn she never listens to you.
2) She speaks so frankly that it hurts.
3) You're so rich!
4) He drank so much coffee that he couldn't sleep.
5) Her guy is so handsome!
6) They're so unhappy they should get divorced.

138

```
¿QUÉ?
¿CUÁNDO?
¿CUÁNTO?      +   accent when a question
¿QUIÉN?
¿CUÁL?
¿POR QUÉ?
```

¿QUÉ TE PARECE LA IDEA?	What do you think of the idea?
Me parece buena.	I think it's good.
La idea me parece buena.	The idea seems good to me.

note: Parece nuevo = It looks new.

¿LE PARECE BIEN (A VD.)?	Does it seem all right to you?
Sí, me parece bien.	Yes, it seems all right to me.
No, no me parece bien.	No, it doesn't seem all right to me.

¿LE ENCANTA LA IDEA?	Do you like (are you pleased with) the idea?
Sí, me encanta.	Yes, I like the idea.
No, no me encanta.	No, I don't like the idea.

PERO, SINO	=	BUT, BUT ONLY
Mi marido es un hombre nervioso <u>pero</u> no es un canalla.		My husband is a nervous man <u>but</u> not a bastard.
Mi marido no es un canalla <u>sino</u> un hombre nervioso.		My husband isn't a bastard <u>but</u> only a nervous man.

note: 'Sino' is used following a negative first clause.

translate:

1) ¿Qué les parece su marido?
2) ¿Le encanta el avión?
3) No sé si volverá o no.
4) ¿Cuándo va a hacerse rico?
5) Quiero algo de beber pero no quiero un café.
6) Le encantan los pasteles.
7) ¿Les gustan los plátanos a los monos?

translate:

1) Do journalists like to make trips?
2) We don't know if he wants to go or not.
3) It seems good to me if we go now.
4) Do you like the idea?
5) She's not really a hooker but only a liberated (free) woman.
6) Do you know whether or not he agrees?
7) They like to dance a lot but on the other hand they don't like modern dances.

VOCABULARIO

	traducción	sinónimo asociado	opuesto asociado
1. alquilar	to rent	arrendar = to sublet	
2. (el) propietario	owner	(el) dueño	(el) inquilino = tenant
3. (el) método	method	(la) manera = way; (el) sistema = system	
4. /bailar/contar	/to dance/to sing	(el) estilo = style	
5. de moda	fashionable ≠ old-fashioned	apreciado, muy chic, muy a la última moda, moderno = modern	pasado de moda, anticuado
6. (la) palabra	word	(la) frase = sentence, (la) página = page	
7. (el) gas	gas	(el) petroleo = oil	
8. escaso	scarce ≠ plentiful	poco, justo	abundante
9. (el) ruido	noise	(el) jaleo, alboroto = racket	(el) silencio
10. /en autobús /en coche	/by bus /by car	en avión = by plane	
11. en vano	in vain, useless	en balde, inútil	útil = useful
12. deber	to owe		to lend = prestar
13. ocasionar	to cause	provocar = to bring on	resultar = to result in
14. ¡es el colmo!	that beats all!	¡es el no va más!	
15. (el) primo	sucker	(el) chupón	
16. absurdo	absurd	ridículo = ridiculous	lógico = logical
17. negocios	business	hacer negocios = to do business	
18. hacerse	to become	volverse, ponerse, llegar a = succeed in	
19. astuto	shrewd, sly	hábil, listo mañoso, retorcido, zorro	
20. ¡sin falta!	without fail!		
21. le advierto	I warn you	amenazar = to threaten	

LECCIÓN 29

AÚN MÁS = STILL MORE = **TODAVÍA MÁS**

Es eso $\dfrac{\text{aún más}}{\text{todavía más}}$ **caro?**   Is this (one) <u>still more</u> expensive?

Si, eso es $\dfrac{\text{aún más}}{\text{todavía más}}$ **caro?**   Yes, this one is <u>still more</u> expensive.

HABRÁ   =   THERE WILL BE

¿Habrá mucha gente en la fiesta?   <u>Will there be</u> many people at the party?

Sí, habrá mucha gente en la fiesta.   Yes, <u>there will be</u> many people at the party.

Sí habrá mucha.   Yes, <u>there will be</u> many.

HABÍA   =   THERE WAS/WERE

¿Había mucha gente?   <u>Were there</u> many people?

Sí, había mucha gente.   Yes, <u>there were</u> many people.
Sí, habí mucha.   Yes, <u>there were</u> many.

VOLVER A	= . . . . . . AGAIN
Vuelvo a hacerlo.	I'm going to do it <u>again</u>.
Volví a llamarle.	I called him <u>again</u>.
¿Cuándo volveré a verle?	When am I sorry to see you <u>again</u>?

note: volver a casa = to return home.

IMPORTAR A	= BE IMPORTANT/MATTER
¿Te importa (a tí)?	Is it <u>important for you</u>?/Does it
¿Le importa (a Vd.)?	<u>matter</u> to you?
Sí, me importa.	Yes, <u>it matters</u>.
No, no me importa.	No, <u>it doesn't matter</u>.

QUERER = TO WANT	QUERER A = TO LOVE
Quiero un café.	**Quiero a María.**
<u>I want</u> a coffee.	<u>I love</u> Maria.

TRAER/LLEVAR	= TO BRING
¿Puede traerme un vaso?	Can you <u>bring me a glass</u>?
Puede llevarla consigo.	You can <u>bring her</u> with you

note: to bring someone = llevar; to bring something = traer.

APOCOPATION!!		
el primer_ año	=	the first year
un mal_ tiempo	=	a bad climate
algun_ pueblo	=	some town
ningun_ padre	=	no father
un buen_ hombre	=	a good man

note: Some adjectives drop the 'o' when placed before a masculine singular noun (not after).

143

translate:

1) ¿Es este coche aún más caro que el otro? Sí, ése es aún más caro.
2) ¿Le importa a Vd. trabajar fuera?
3) Sí, me importa porque es aún más difícil.
4) Había muchos pasajeros encantados con el viaje.
5) ¿Puede traerme una copa por favor?
6) No sé conducir un coche, en cambio sé montar a caballo.
7) ¿Puedo llevarla conmigo esta noche?
8) ¿Le importa a Vd. si comemos juntos en este sitio tranquilo?
9) Vuelvo más tarde, entonces volveré a llamarle luego.
10) Quiero un té.
11) Quiero a mi marido más que a mis críos.
12) ¿Es este tío mas coño que el otro? Si, es todavía más coño.
13) ¿Les importa a Vds. ir ahora mismo?
14) Voy a bailar aunque estoy cansada.

translate:

1) We're going to do the work again.
2) Do you love her?
3) You can bring him with you if you want.
4) There were a lot of people at the cinema (US: movies).
5) Is this thing still more expensive than the other one?
6) It doesn't matter.
7) The point is that, although I drive, I don't want to take my car.
8) Even the passengers were afraid.
9) There will be a crowd in the house.
10) The owner is bringing his brother.
11) Does it matter to them if they work at night?
12) The underworld is going to try to kill him again.
13) Do you love money?
14) Yes, but even so, I wouldn't kill for it.

144

VOCABULARIO

	traducción	sinónimo asociado	opuesto asociado
1. enorme	huge ≠ tiny	grandísimo, desmesurado	pequeñín, chiquitín
2. /(el) extranjero /(el) desconocido	/foreigner /stranger	fuera = abroad	
3. /franco/francamente	/frank/frankly	sinceramente = honestly	andarse por las ramas = to beat around the bush
4. (la) costumbre	habit	(el) hábito	
5. imaginar	to imagine	hacer como si = to pretend, fingir	
6. conducir	to drive	manejar, montar a caballo = to ride a horse	
7. aumentar	to increase ≠ to decrease, to go down	subir = to go up	caer, decrecer, bajar
8. me va bien	it fits me, suits me	/me conviene/me sienta bien	ancho = loose, apretado = tight
9. soler	to be used to	tener la costumbre de = acostumbrarse	hacerse = to get used to
10. (la) ocasión	chance, opportunity	(la) oportunidad	
11. amable	friendly	cariñoso	frío = cold
12. (el) pasajero	passenger		(el) conductor
13. (la) pausa	break	(la) tregua	
14. el caso es que	the point is	la cosa está en que	no es el caso = that's not the point
15. quieto	calm	tranquilo, sosegado	
16. encantado	delighted, thrilled		desilusionado = disappointed
17. /aún/aún cuando	/still, even/even so, even if (note: still sick = todavía enferma ≠ no more = ya no)	aún yo = hasta yo = even me; aún mas caro = still (even) more expensive; todavía más/aunque = although	

145

LECCIÓN 30

REFLEXIVE VERBS

LAVARSE = TO GET WASHED (WASH ONESELF)

me lavo   I'm getting washed
te lavas
se lava

nos lavamos
os laváis
Vds. se lavan

note: — Reflexive verbs are extremely frequent in Spanish.
       — when used with the infinitive, the reflexive is attached:
          quiero lavar**me** = I want to wash (myself).

¿TE LAVAS CADA DÍA?	Do you wash every day?
Sí, me lavo cada día.	Yes, I wash every day.
No, no me lavo cada día.	No, I don't wash every day.

SOME REFLEXIVE VERBS

sentarse	to sit down	**equivocarse**	to make a mistake
ponerse de pie	to stand up	**pasearse**	to go for a walk
levantarse	to get up	**vestirse**	to dress
acostarse	to go to bed	**enfermarse**	to become ill
llamarse	to be called	**quejarse**	to complain
encontrarse	to be at	**ponerse, hacerse,**	to become
	(to find someone at)	**volverse**	
comerse	to eat up	**quitarse**	to take off one's
llevarse	/to take away		clothes
	/to get along	**preocuparse**	to worry about
irse	to go away	**cansarse**	to get tired
acordarse	to remember	**quedarse**	to stay, remain
ponerse	to become/get	**enfriarse**	to catch cold
enojarse	to get angry	**sentirse**	to feel (sick)
divertirse	to have a good time	**aburrirse**	to be bored
arreglarse	to get ready	**despedirse**	to be off, leave
bañarse	/to swim/to take a	**acostumbrarse**	to get used to
	bath	**caerse**	to fall down
enterarse	to find out	**figurarse**	to imagine
retrasarse	to be late	**casarse**	to get married
jactarse	to boast	**atreverse**	to dare to
traerse	to bring, carry	**alegrarse**	to be glad about
encargarse	to take care of	**presentarse**	to show up, come
ahorrarse	to save	**distraerse**	to have fun
asustarse	to get frightened	**mejorarse**	to get better
decidirse	to make up one's	**ponerse**	to put on (clothes)
	mind	**divorciarse**	to get divorced
darse prisa	to hurry up	**darse cuenta**	to realise
separarse	to take leave, say		
	good-bye		

SE	= EACH OTHER
Se hablaban.	They were talking to each other.
Nos vemos a menudo.	We see each other often.
Nos queremos.	We love each other.

147

translate:

1) Se equivoca a menudo.
2) Se acuerda de sus últimas vacaciones.
3) ¿Te llamas Perez?
4) Me aburro por lo que dice.
5) ¿Se queja a menudo?
6) Van a divorciarse este año.
7) ¿Os casáis el mes próximo?
8) ¿Te desvistes delante de tu marido?
9) ¿Se pasean a veces los fines de semana?
10) ¿Te levantas temprano cada mañana?
11) Se divierten mucho por la noche.
12) ¿Cómo te sientes?
13) Nos enfríamos mucho en invierno.
14) Tu padre no se enfada nunca con tus hermanos.

translate:

1) I'm washing and getting dressed and ready for the party.
2) We're wondering where you wanted to go.
3) He's going to become a doctor soon.
4) We'll have a great time tonight.
5) I make mistakes all the time.
6) Do you realise what you're saying?
7) If you want to, we'll go for a walk.
8) If you don't go to sleep early, you'll never get up on time.
9) Why don't you put on a coat?
10) I don't remember his face.
11) He's always complaining.
12) I can't get used to his smoking.
13) I don't care about what you say.
14) Hurry up, we're late.

VOCABULARIO

	traducción	sinónimo asociado	opuesto asociado
1. es un alivio	it's a relief	es un descanso	
2. (el) jabón/(la) toalla/(el) cepillo de dientes	/soap/towel /toothbrush	pasta de dientes = toothpaste	
3. /practicamente todo/tanto	/practically all /so very much	casi del todo = nearly all, todo lo que = all that; aún más que = even more than	de ninguna manera = not at all, ¡tan poco! = so little!
4. /(la) manta/(la) almohada	/blanket/pillow	(la) sábana = sheet	
5. /en cualquier momento/en cualquier sitio /cualquier cosa	/whenever/wherever /whatever	lo que sea; cada vez que = every time	
6. (la) conversación	conversation	charlar = to chat	
7. realizarse	to come true	llegar a ser verdad	
8. tener enchufe	to have contacts	relaciones = connections	
9. permanente	permanent	duradero	temporal = temporary
10. /(el) árbol/(la) flor/(el) jardin /(el) patio	/tree/flower/garden /yard	(el) parque = park; (la) selva, (el) bosque = forest; (la) hierba = grass	
11. /(el) cielo/(las) estrellas	/sky/stars	(la) luna = moon	
12. (el) rascacielos	skyscraper	(la) vista = sight	
13. más lejos	further	en la lejanía	más cerca = nearer
14. cotilleo	gossip	chismes	
15. fresco	fresh	reciente	rancio = stale
16. fuera	outside ≠ indoor		dentro
17. desmayarse	to faint	marearse	
18. tal como	as is	tal cual	
19. ¡oye!	listen	¡oiga!, ¡escuche!	¡diga!
20. reparar	to repair, fix ≠ break	arreglar, fijar	romper

149

LECCIÓN 31

YO MISMO	= MYSELF	
yo mismo	myself	
tú mismo	yourself	
él mismo	himself	
ella misma	herself	**Lo haré yo mismo.**
sí mismo	oneself	I'll do it myself.
Vd. mismo	yourself	
nosotros(as) mismos(as)	ourselves	**Se vistió ella misma.**
vosotros(as) mismos(as)	yourselves	She got dressed herself
ellos(as) mismos(as)	themselves	
Vds. mismos	yourselves	

note: I did it myself = lo hice yo mismo = lo hice solo = I did it alone.

¿LO HA HECHO ELLA MISMA?	Did she do it herself?
Sí, lo ha hecho ella misma.	Yes, she did it herself.
No, no lo ha hecho ella misma.	No, she didn't do it herself.

note: 'yo mismo' can be replaced by 'por mí mismo', e.g. lo he hecho por mí mismo = I did it myself = yo mismo.

Insert the correct reflexive pronoun:

1) ¿Ha escrito su libro . . . . . . ?
2) Sé que lo has hecho . . . .
3) ¿Ha pagado sus impuestos . . . . . . ?
4) El jefe ha contradado a su secretaria . . . .
5) Los obreros . . . se han puesto en huelga.
6) Se arregló . . . . . . para no trabajar los fines de semana.
7) Nosotros . . . hemos preparado la comida.
8) El director no ha tomado los riesgos . . . .
9) Organizó . . . . . . la fiesta.
10) Esta fabrica hace . . . . . . los productos que vende.

150

VERBOS REFLEXIVOS (reflexive verbs) — PRETÉRITO (past)

me lavé ayer	I got washed yesterday
te lavaste ayer	you got washed
se lavó ayer	he/she/you got washed
nos lavamos ayer	we got washed
os lavásteis ayer	you got washed
se lavaron ayer	they/you got washed

note: The alternative form — me he lavado — is less often used.

¿SE FUÉ DE PASEO AYER?	Did you go for a walk yesterday?
Sí, me fuí de paseo ayer.	Yes, I went for a walk yesterday.
No, no me fuí de paseo ayer.	No, I didn't go for a walk yesterday.

translate and put into the present:

1) You got excited yesterday, and you're getting excited again today.
2) She didn't realize that her husband was lying.
3) The girls went upstairs to get undressed and to wash.
4) We talk to each other every week.
5) We woke up late on vacation, and now we wake up early for work.
6) I didn't make mistakes yesterday and I'm not making mistakes now.
7) What time did you go to bed last night.
8) I didn't remember her husband or the kids either
9) We had a good time last night, and we always have a good time.
10) I hurried up but you didn't realize that I wanted to see you sooner.
11) She got married again, I wonder if she remembers all her husbands.
12) The teacher gets angry and gets tired easily.
13) I took off my old coat and put on my new one.
14) We started to work and then realized how glad we were to be able to do it all without making a mistake.

VOCABULARIO

	traducción	sinónimo asociado	opuesto asociado
1. fabricar	to manufacture	hacer = to make	
2. (la) reunión	meeting	(el) mitín; (el) líder = leader	
3. (la) fábrica	factory	(la) empresa	
4. (el) mercado	market	(la) plaza	
5. organizar	to organize	establecer	proporcionar = to supply
6. al por menor	retail ≠ wholesale	(el) detalle	al por mayor
7. contratar	to hire ≠ to fire	(el) personal = staff	despedir
8. /(el) ingeniero /(el) puente	/engineer/bridge	(el) edificio = building	
9. ¡entendido!	it's a deal!	poner un negocio = to put a deal together	
10. construir	to build	edificar	to destroy = destruir
11. (la) máquina	machine	ordenador = computer = computadora	
12. (el) anuncio	ad, a commercial	hacer publicidad = to advertise	
13. ¿por qué no?	why not?		
14. (el) cliente	client ≠ salesman		(el) vendedor
15. /(la) renta /impuestos	/income/taxes	ingreso	
16. (el) sueldo	salary, pay	(la) paga, (el) salario	
17. /(el) riesgo /arriesgado	risk, risky	atrevido; tentar la suerte = take a chance	está en el bote = it's a sure thing
18. pretende que	he claims that	intenta que	
19. se las arregló	he swung it (arreglarse = to swing, manage)	llegó a = he managed to; alcanzar, conseguir	
20. (el) estado	state	(el) país = country	

LECCIÓN 32

VERB REVISION:

PRESENTE (present)

a menudo.	<u>often</u>.
Trabajo <u>**todos los días.**</u>	I work <u>every day</u>,
<u>**algunas veces.**</u>	<u>sometimes</u>.

Trabaj<u>o</u> <u>ahora</u> = **<u>Estoy</u> trabaj<u>ando</u> <u>ahora</u>** = I'm working <u>now</u>.
(in the midst of)

FUTURO (future)

<u>**mañana.**</u>	<u>tomorrow</u>.
Trabajar<u>é</u> <u>la semana próxima.</u>	I'<u>ll</u> work <u>next week</u>.
<u>**dentro de dos horas.**</u>	<u>in two hours</u>.

PRETÉRITO (past)

<u>**ayer.**</u>	<u>yesterday</u>.
Trabaj<u>é</u> <u>la semana pasada.</u>	I work<u>ed</u> <u>last week</u>.
<u>**hace dos días.**</u>	<u>two days ago</u>.

note: This past denotes a finished action and a specified time.

IMPERFECTO (imperfect)

Trabaj<u>aba</u> <u>**cuando vino.**</u>	I <u>was</u> working <u>when</u> he came.
<u>**mientras comía.**</u>	<u>while</u> you were eating.

note: Distinguish between — I worked yesterday = trabaj<u>é</u> ayer.
— I was working <u>when</u> . . . = trabaj<u>aba</u> cuando . . .
(an action <u>going on when</u> . . .)

PRETÉRITO INDEFINIDO (indefinite past)

He traba<u>jado</u> mucho.   I <u>have worked</u> a lot.

note: This is for the past when you don't know 'when' — it is less often used than the 'real' past.

SI = IF

Si <u>tengo</u> dinero, <u>compraré</u> un coche.
If I have the money, I'll buy a car.

Si <u>tuviera</u> dinero, <u>compraría</u> un coche.
If I had the money, I would buy a car.

Si <u>hubiera tenido</u> dinero, <u>hubiera comprado</u> un coche.
If I had had the money, I would have bought a car.

THE KILLER!!

REMEMBER — A PAST WHICH CONTINUES

I <u>have been living</u> here for two years.

Vivo aquí <u>desde hace</u> dos años.
<u>Hace</u> dos años que <u>vivo</u> aquí.
Estoy viviendo aquí <u>desde hace</u> dos años.

insert the correct tense (the pronouns in square brackets are for guidance in choosing the correct verb form only):

1) Nos . . . (pasearse) juntos ayer.
2) ¿[tú] . . . (hacer) la comida mañana? [yo] . . . (hacer) ayer.
3) [Vd.] . . . (mirar) la tele desde hace dos horas.
4) ¿[vosotros] . . . (ir) al cine hace dos semanas?
5) [él] . . . (leer) mientras [tú] . . . (dormir).
6) [él] . . . (reñir) desde hace una hora.
7) ¿[tú] . . . (estar) ya en Inglaterra?
8) ¿Desde cuándo [Vd.] . . . (estar) aquí?
9) [él] . . . (conducir) cuando el accidente . . . (occurir).
10) [ellos] . . . (estar casado) desde hace dos años.
11) [ella] . . . (dormir) a pesar de la lluvia.
12) Cuando la policía . . . (llegar), los gamberros . . . (robar) ya mucho.
13) [yo] . . . pensar que [tu] . . . (salir) desde hace una hora.
14) [yo] . . . (aprender) español desde hace un año.
15) ¿[tú] . . . (ver) ya esta película?
16) [yo] . . . (tener que) ir con él ayer.
17) Qué . . . (hacer) Vd. cuando [yo] . . . (entrar).
18) [ella] . . . (estar infeliz) desde su boda.
19) [nosotros] . . . (empezar) otra lección mañana.
20) [yo] . . . (poder) hacerlo ayer y no . . . (poder) hacerlo mañana.
21) [yo] . . . (tratar de) llamarle desde esta mañana.
22) [nosotros]. . . (hacer la comida) cuando [él] . . . (entrar) a casa.
23) [ellos] . . . (lavarse) esta mañana. Nos (lavar) cada día.
24) [tú] . . . (recordar) lo que [él] . . . (decir) cuando le [nosotros] . . . (encontrar) la semana pasada.
25) Me [él] . . . (decir) lo mismo desde ayer.
26) [yo] . . . (ser) profesor en Madrid antes de . . . (ir) a los Estados Unidos.
27) [ellos] . . . (divorciarse) hace seis meses. ¿Desde cuándo . . . (divorciarse) Vd.?
28) [nosotros] . . . (arreglarse) el coche . . . (romper).

translate, then give the second and third form of IF:

1) If I can, I'll go with you.
2) If you don't get undressed, I'll beat you.
3) If they love each other, why don't they get married?
4) If you get angry again, I'll leave you.
5) If we don't have to do the work now, we'll go for a walk.
6) If he doesn't work, he won't pass his exam.
7) If they're rich next year, they'll buy another house.
8) If we can help, we'll call you.
9) If you want to sell your car, I'll buy it.
10) If he's an ass his broad won't love him.
11) If the cops can catch the gangster, they'll put him in jail.
12) If your sister takes the pill, she won't get pregnant.
13) If she wants to have an abortion, the doctor will do it.
14) If the workers go on strike, the unions will be happy.
15) If there's another war, we'll all be killed.
16) If you don't stop complaining, I'll scream.
17) If you want to take a trip, I'll come with you.
18) If politicians don't take bribes, that will be amazing.
19) If we have to pay out taxes early, we'll be in a jam.
20) If we don't take the highway, the trip will take longer.
21) If soldiers refuse to go to war, the world will at last be happy.
22) If his policy is so stupid, we won't vote for him.
23) If I have to lose weight, I'll try to go on a diet.
24) If the guy's crazy, he'll become a soldier.
25) If you recognize him, you will be lucky.
26) If the weather's bad, we'll stay inside.
27) If you don't want to stay here alone, I'll leave the kids with you.
28) If you continue to worry so much about him, I'll begin to think you're in love with him.

translate:

1) They've been engaged since Christmas. Do you think they're going to get married soon?
2) I was laughing while you were getting angry.
3) You should give her a gift for this birthday and you should have given her one last year.
4) I've been trying for two hours to call you.
5) I was wondering if you're coming.
6) I don't see anyone and I don't hear anything.
7) I have only a little dough. Can you lend me some?
8) Our company has been supplying the factory with computers for years and years.
9) He didn't understand anything. He never understand anything.
10) I was getting divorced when I met him.
11) I'm trying to understand you.
12) You don't have to take your own soap with you.
13) Why are you so angry? I am not complaining.
14) The crooks were robbing the bank when the cops came.
15) You shouldn't have taken these drugs.
16) I can't help it. I'm too tired.
17) He's been hitting his wife since their baby was born.
18) For how long have you been pregnant?
19) My leg has been hurting me since the accident.
20) Would you mind if I smoked while you're eating?
21) I had to leave a big tip. You should have left one too.
22) I couldn't stay honest in politics, could you?
23) The underworld is so strong that we're all afraid.
24) For how long have you been married?
25) Did you know he was making love with his secretary while you were on your trip?
26) You should have got used to his jokes a long time ago.
27) You should have told me earlier that you weren't going to come.
28) We were paying high taxes and we were going broke at the same time.

translate:

1) You've been cooking the same dish since this morning.
2) He's a fairy and his sister's a hooker.
3) Do you need help?
4) My arm has been hurting me all day.
5) I'm going to get washed and dressed and ready to go out.
6) She lived in New York for ten years when she was young and now she's been living in Madrid for two years.
7) Do you realize how stupid they are?
8) I didn't remember his name. You must ask him it.
9) They've been selling retail since Christmas.
10) We've been manufacturing computers for a long time.
11) I have to tell you something important.
12) She was trying to help him but he got angry.
13) You should have gone with me yesterday. You never listen when I tell you you should go with me.
14) I didn't have to do it for today. I have to do it for tomorrow.
15) They were stealing the lot when the cops came in.
16) She's not here. She must be sick.
17) You have to give bribes if you want the help of politicians.
18) I couldn't go with you yesterday, but I could have gone the day before.
19) You should have called and told me you were in a jam.
20) He didn't know what to do, so I told him that he should see the boss.
21) If you were one of his friends, you would be used to drinking a lot too.
22) What a sucker you are! You shouldn't have believed him.
23) I couldn't bear him, and I don't understand how she can love him.
24) You had to be a fool to believe everything the politician said.
25) He was going to retire when his kids got sick.
26) I don't have to help you as you didn't help me when I needed it.
27) He can come if he wants to. It doesn't matter to me.
28) I don't give a darn! He can go to hell!

VOCABULARIO (a)

	traducción	sinónimo asociado	opuesto asociado
1. a principios de	at the beginning of	(el) comienzo = the beginning	a finales de = at the end of, (el) fin = the end
2. los gastos	expenses	(la) factura = bill	
3. el fin de semana	weekend		
4. (el) asunto	matter, subject	(la) cuestión	
5. /(el) deporte /(el) equipo/jugar	/sports/team/to play	(el) béisbol = baseball, ( ) fútbol = footbaı	tocar = to play (musical instrument)
6. usar	to use	utilizar	
7. a ver	let's see	vamos a ver	
8. cambiar	to change		
9. gastar	to spend ≠ save		ahorrar
10. (la) entrevista	interview	(el) empleo = (el) puesto = employment	
11. en la esquina	on the corner	(el) barrio = area	
12. ¡no tarde!	don't be long		
13. tan pronto como	as soon as	luego que, así que	
14. /(la) obra de teatro/(el) actor /(el) teatro	/play/actor/theatre	/(la) comedia/(la) actriz (desempeñar = to act); hacer un papel = to play a role	
15. /(la) escena/(el) escenógrafo	/stage/director		
16. de memoria	by heart		
17. /lo mejor es/lo bueno es que	/the best thing is /the good thing is		lo malo es que = the bad thing is
18. los demás	the others	los otros (los demás = the rest − something)	
19. ¿cuánto tiempo duró?	how long did it last?		
20. /dejar un recado /volver a llamar	/to leave a message /to call back	(el) número de teléfono = phone number; (la) dirección = las señas = address	

VOCABULARIO (b)

	traducción	sinónimo asociado	opuesto asociado
1. /(la) promesa/(el) secreto	/promise/secret		
2. /(la) pista/(el) indicio	/tip/clue	(el) bulo, alduir = to hint	
3. /pasar un examen /aprobar un examen	/to take a test /to pass a test		
4. (la) recompensa	reward	(el) premio	
5. /(la) carretera /(la) autopista	/road/highway	(el) camino = path	
6. querido	darling	mi vida, (el) amante (lover)	
7. (un) maricón	gay, queer ≠ dyke	(la) marica	(la) lesbiana, (la) tortillera
8. perjudicar	to damage	hacer daño = to harm = dañar; lastimar = to injure	
9. (la) paz	peace ≠ war		(la) guerra = army; (el) ejército; (el) soldado = soldier
10. cocinar	to cook	hervir = to boil; asar = to roast; freir = to fry	
11. /coser/(la) aguja	/to sew/needle	(el) hilo = thread; (la) plancha = iron; lavar = to wash	
12. practicar	to practise	ejercitarse = hacer exercicios	
13. reconocer	to recognise		
14. ¡vete al diablo!	go to hell!	¡vete a la mierda!	
15. hacer el amor	to make love	joder = to screw = coger	
16. /(el) rey/(la) reina	/king/queen	(el) príncipe = prince	
17. /volver/volver a	/to return/to do		
18. me importa un carajo	I don't give a damn!, a darn!	me importa un pito = un bledo = un comino	
19. (la) puta	hooker	prostituta	

160

VERBOS Y PREPOSICIONES
(VERBS AND PREPOSITIONS) 1

a) fill in the blanks in the second column as far as you can;
b) fold the page back to check your answer;
c) read the translation of the sentence for further clarification.

1. to enter	Entró . . . la casa.
2. *a.* to speak to/to talk to	— Quisiera hablar . . . el Señor Perez.
b. to speak about	— Estábamos hablando . . . tí.
3. to depend on	Depende . . . Vd.
4. to agree with	Estoy de acuerdo . . . Vd.
5. /to be interested in ≠ bored by	Estoy interesado . . . mi trabajo. ≠ aburrido . . .
6. to live in	Vive . . . Madrid.
7. to be married to	Se casó . . . un americano.
8. to go to	Fué . . . Nueva York el año pasado.
9. whose is it?	¿ . . . quién es este perro? (but: it belongs to me = es mío)
10. to be mad at	Estoy enfadado . . . él.
11. to be sick of	Estoy harto . . . verla triste.
12. to be worried about	Estoy preocupado . . . su salud.
13. *a.* to get used to	— Nunca me acostumbraré . . . su manera de hablar.
b. to be used to	— ¿Te has acostumbrado . . . ?
14. before ≠ after	Antes . . . ≠ después . . . comer, fuimos al ciné.
15. to go out of	Salió . . . casa.
16. in front of ≠ behind	Anda delante . . . sus hijos. ≠ detrás.. . .
17. to try to	Trate . . . hacerlo, por favor.
18. to begin again ≠ to stop	Volvió . . . fumar. ≠ Cesó . . . fumar. Dejó . . .
19. to come back	Volvió . . . casa.
20. to be about to	Estamos . . . irnos.
21. to leave with	Puede dejar los niños . . . migo.

VERBOS Y PREPOSICIONES 1

1. entrar en	He entered the house.
2. *a.* **hablar con**	— I would like to speak to Mr Perez.
b. **hablar de**	— We were speaking about you.
3. depende de	It depends on you.
4. estar de acuerdo con	I agree with you.
5. estar interesado por	I'm interested in my book.
≠ **aburrido por**	bored by
6. vivir en	He lives in Madrid.
7. casarse con	She married an American.
8. ir a	He went to New York last year.
9. ¿de quién es?	Who does this dog belong to?
10. estar enfadado con	I'm mad at him.
11. estar harto de	I'm sick of seeing her sad.
12. estar preocupado por	I'm worried about his health.
13. *a.* **acostumbrarse a**	— I'll never get used to his way of speaking.
b. **estar acostum-**	— Are you used to getting up early?
brado a	
14. antes de ≠ después	Before ≠ after eating, we went to the cinema.
de	
15. salir de	He went out of the house.
16. delante de/detrás de	He's walking in front of ≠ behind his children.
17. tratar de	Please, try to do it.
18. volver a ≠ dejar	He began to smoke again ≠ He stopped smoking.
de/cesar de	
19. volver a	He came back home.
20. estar por	We're about to go.
21. dejar con	You can leave the kids with me.

VERBS AND PREPOSITIONS 2

1. to explain to | Voy a explicar . . . mi amigo. (or: voy a explicarle)
2. to get in ≠ to get out | Sube . . . coche.
   | ≠ Sal . . .
3. to laugh at | No te rías . . . mí.
4. on behalf of | Le llamo de parte . . . María.
5. near ≠ far from | Vive cerca . . . mí.
   | ≠ lejos . . .
6. to write to | He escrito una carta . . . mi padre. (or: le he escrito)
7. to be about | ¿ . . . que se trata?
8. to realize | No me dí cuenta . . . problema.
9. as for (me) | . . . mí, no está de acuerdo con Vd.
10. to have just | Acaba . . . salir.
11. to love someone | Quiero mucho . . . mi madre.
12. to count on | Cuento mucho . . . Vd.
13. to invite to | Te invito . . . la fiesta.
14. to refuse to | Se negó . . . hacerlo.
15. instead of | Quiere un café en vez . . . un té.
16. to intend to | Tenemos la intención . . . ir al extranjero este verano.
17. to give to | Dió una muñeca . . . su prima.
18. in spite of | A pesar . . . eso, lo hizo.
19. *a.* to be glad to | — Estoy contenta . . . marcharme. (or: Me alegro . . .)
    b. to enjoy | — Gozó . . . está película.
20. to remember ≠ to forget | ¿Te acuerdas . . . mí o te has olvidado . . . mí?
21. to come to | ¿Cuando vienes . . . casa?
22. *a.* to manage to | — Llegó . . . ser médico.
    b. to arrive | — El tren llega . . . las doce.
23. to answer | ¿Por qué no me contestas . . . mí?
24. to take advantage of | Aprovéchese . . . este buen tiempo para ir a pasearse.

VERBOS Y PREPOSICIÓNES 2

1. explicar a	I'm going to explain it to my friends.
2. subir en/salir de	Get in ≠ Get out of the car.
3. reirse de	Don't laugh at me.
4. de parte de	I'm calling you on behalf of Mary.
5. cerca de ≠ lejos de	He lives near me ≠ far from me.
6. escribir a	I wrote to my father.
7. ¿de qué se trata?	What is it about?
8. darse cuenta de	I didn't realise the problem.
9. para mí . . .	As for me, I don't agree with you.
10. acabar de	He had just left.
11. querer a	I love my mother.
12. contar con	I'm counting a lot on you.
13. invitar a alguien	I'm inviting you to the party.
14. negarse en	He refused to do it.
15. en vez de	I want coffee instead of tea.
16. tener la intención de	We intend to go abroad this summer.
17. dar a alguien	He gave a doll to his cousin.
18. a pesar de	In spite of that he did it.
19. *a.* **estar contento de/ alegrarse de**	— I'm glad to go.
b. **gozar de**	— I enjoyed the film.
20. acordarse de alguien ≠ olvidarse de	Do you remember me or did you forget me?
21. venir a	When will you come to our house?
22. llegar a	— He managed to be a doctor. — The train arrived at noon.
23. contestar a	Why don't you answer me?
24. aprovecharse de	Take advantage of the nice weather and go for a walk.

VERBS AND PREPOSITIONS 3

1. to wait for   **Esperé . . . mi hermana todo el día.**

2. *a.* to learn to   **— Aprendemos . . . hablar español.**
   b. to teach   **— La maestra nos enseña . . . hablar.**

3. to listen to   **Durante la clase, escuchamos . . . la profesora.**

4. to call up   **Me llamó . . . mí esta mañana.**

5. to doubt   **Dudo . . . su sinceridad.**

6. most of   **La mayoría . . . la gente ha venido.**

7. in addition   **Además . . . ser inteligente, es guapa.**

8. to look like   **Se parece mucho . . . su padre.**

9. *a.* to think about   **— Piensa . . . lo que dijo.**
         something
   b. to think about   **— Pienso . . . tí.**
         someone
   c. to think about   **— ¿Qué piensas . . . lo que dijo?**
         (opinion)
   d. to think about   **— ¿ . . . qué piensas?**
         (in general)

10. concerning, relating   **El jefe quiere verle a propósito . . . las huelgas.**
        to

11. to have a part in the   **¿Está interesado . . . este negocio?**
        business

12. to be good at   **Está fuerte . . . matématicas.**

13. to take care of   **Me ocuparé . . . problema.**

14. to be ashamed of   **Tiene vergüenza . . . su mujer.**
    ≠ to be proud of   **≠ Está orgulloso.**

15. to be afraid of   **Tengo miedo . . . tí.**

16. to feel like   **¿Tiene ganas . . . un café?**

17. /to start/begin   **Vamos a empezar . . . trabajar mañana.**
    ≠ to finish   **principiar . . .**
                          echar . . .
                          comenzar . . .
               ≠ Vamos a acabar . . . trabajar mañana.
                          terminar . . .

18. under   **El gato está debajo . . . la mesa.**

19. /to ask someone for   **Pedí dinero . . . Pedro/Quiero preguntarle algo . . .**
        something/to ask   **Vd.**
        someone something

165

VERBOS Y PREPOSICIÓNES 3

1. esperar a	I waited for my sister all day.
2. *a.* **aprender a**	— We're learning to speak Spanish.
b. **enseñar a**	— The teacher is teaching us to speak.
3. escuchar a	During the class, we listen to the teacher.
4. llamar a	He called me this morning.
5. dudar a	I doubt his sincerity.
6. la mayoría de	Most of the people came.
7. además de	She's intelligent and beautiful in addition.
8. parecerse a	He looks like his father.
9. *a.* **pensar en**	— Think about what he said.
b. **pensar en**	— I'm thinking about you.
c. **pensar de**	— What do you think about it?
d. **pensar en**	— What are you thinking about?
10. a propósito de	The boss wants to see you concerning the strikes.
11. estar interesado en	Have you a part in the business?
12. estar fuerte en	He's good at maths.
13. ocuparse de	I'll take care of the problem.
14. tener vergüenza de	He's ashamed of his wife.
≠ **estar orgulloso de**	≠ proud
15. tener miedo de	I'm afraid of you.
16. tener ganas de	Do you feel like a coffee?
17. /empezar a	We're going to start the work tomorrow.
/principiar a/echar	≠ finish
a/comenzar a ≠	
acabar de/terminar	
de	
18. debajo de	The cat's under the table.
19. /pedir algo a alguien	/I asked him for some money./I want to ask you
/preguntar algo a	something.
alguien	

THE CASE OF THE MISSING PREPOSITIONS, ETC. !!!

1. I'm looking for the same one.	Busco el mismo.
2. Look at this.	Mira eso.
3. How much did you pay for it?	¿Cuánto lo has pagado?
4. I'll try to come.	Intento venir.
5. He came back late.	Volvió muy tarde.
6. Put on ≠ Take off your coat.	Pon ≠ quítate este abrigo.
7. I have to go.	Tengo que ir./Hay que ir.
8. /to get up/to wake up	/levantarse/despertarse
9. to sit down ≠ to stand up	sentarse ≠ ponerse de pie
10. He went on talking.	Siguió hablando.
11. I'd like to go.	Me gustaría ir.
12. Do you know how to drive?	¿Sabe conducir?
13. I'm able to do it.	Puedo hacerlo.
14. I'm going out now.	Salgo ahora./Me voy.
15. I hope to go.	Espero ir.
16. I want to see it.	Quiero/deseo verlo.
17. I expect to go to Italy.	Espero ir a Italia.
18. I'm used to smoking a lot.	Suelo fumar mucho.
19. I waited for you an hour.	Te esperé una hora.
20. I took it out (of my pocket).	La saqué (de mi bolsillo).
21. Turn on ≠ off the light!	¡Apaga ≠ enciende la luz!
22. What did she have on?	¿Qué llevaba?
23. I'm listening to you.	Le escucho.
24. There were a lot of people there.	Había mucha gente ahí.
25. According to him . . .	Según él . . .
26. Show it to me . . .	Enséñamelo.
27. Bring it to me.	Tráigamelo.
28. It's on top of the table.	Está sobre la mesa.

MODISMOS (IDIOMS)

a) fill in the blanks in the second column as far as you can;
b) fold the page back to check your answer;
c) read the translation of the sentence for further clarification.

IDIOMS 1

1. to go for a walk	¿Nos vamos . . . . . . ? (or: Vamos . . . . . . ?)
2. /I don't care/it doesn't matter	No me . . . .
3. I'd like you to meet . . .	Quiero . . . . . . Jaime./ i . . . !
4. /hurry up!/to be in a hurry	/ ¡Date . . . !/Tengo . . . . (or: Estoy de . . . .)
5. that's the limit	Es el . . . !
6. /to be on the line /hang on!	/El Señor Garcia está . . . ./No . . . !
7. /how are you?/fine, thank you, and you?	/¿Qué . . . ? (or: ¿Cómo . . . ? or: ¿Cómo . . . ?) /¿Bien y . . . ?
8. to make a mistake	Me he . . . .
9. do you have a light?	¿Tiene . . . ?
10. too bad ≠ all the better	¡Tanto . . . ! ≠ ¡Tanto . . . !
11. on the other hand	No es muy inteligente, pero por . . . . . . es agradable.
12. to be fed up	¡Estoy . . . !
13. it isn't worth it	No merece . . . . (or: No . . . .)
14. /how goes it?/not good/not bad	/¿Cómo . . . ? (or: ¿Cómo . . . ? or: ¿Cómo le van . . . . . . ?) /No . . . ./No del . . . .
15. /to have to/must	/Tengo . . . ir./Hay . . . ir.
16. I'm starving ≠ I'm full	Me muero . . . . ≠ Estoy . . . .
17. to do a favour	¿Puede Vd. hacerme un . . . ?
18. to change one's mind	Cambié de . . . .
19. I was wondering	Me . . . lo que diría.
20. to ask questions	Nunca hace . . . .
21. to go shopping	Mañana iremos de . . . . (or: saldremos de . . . .)
22. I don't feel like it	No me da . . . .
23. how much is it?	¿Qué precio . . . ? (or: . . . es? or: . . . ?)

MODISMOS 1

1. irse de paseo (or: ir a pasearse)	Are we going for a walk?
2. no me importa	I don't care!
3. /quiero presentarle a . . . /encantado	/I'd like you to meet James./Pleased to meet you.
4. /darse prisa/tener prisa (or: estar de prisa)	/Hurry up!/I'm in a hurry.
5. ¡es el colmo!	That's the limit!
6. /llamar/ ¡no cuelgue!	/Mr Smith is on the line./Hang on!
7. /¿qué tal? (or: ¿cómo está? or: ¿va?) /¿bien, y Vd.?	/how are you?/Fine, thank you, and you?
8. equivocarse	I made a mistake.
9. ¿tiene fuego?	Do you have a light?
10. ¡tanto peor! ≠ ¡tanto mejor!	Too bad! ≠ All the better?
11. por otro lado	He isn't bright, but on the other hand, he's charming.
12. estar harto	I'm fed up.
13. no vale (or: merece la pena)	It isn't worth it.
14. /¿como anda? (or: ¿va? or: ¿como le van las cosas?)/no va/no del todo mal	/How goes it?/Not well./Not bad.
15. tener que/hay que	I have to go.
16. me muero de hambre ≠ estoy harto	I'm starving ≠ I'm full
17. hacer un favor	Could you please do me a favour?
18. cambiar de idea	I changed my mind.
19. me preguntaba	I was wondering what he would say.
20. hacer preguntas	He never asks questions.
21. ir/salir de compras	Tomorrow, we'll go shopping.
22. no me da la gana	I don't feel like it.
23. ¿qué precio tiene? /¿cuanto es?/¿vale?	How much is it?

IDIOMS 2

1. /I hope so/I think so | /Espero . . . ./Creo . . . .
2. to miss | Te echo . . . .
3. what a pity! | ¡Que . . . ! (or: ¡ . . . !)
4. to shake hands | En España se da la . . . .
5. to make an appointment | Estoy citada . . . mi novio. He hecho . . . . . .
6. to pull someone's leg | ¡No me tome el . . . !
7. to stay a while | ¿Por qué no te quedas . . . . . . ?
8. as for me . . . | En cuanto . . . . . . , no estoy de acuerdo.
9. to have breakfast | Vamos a tomar . . . .
10. /to stand up/to be standing | / ¡Pónte . . . . . . !/Estoy . . . .
11. to be in a good ≠ bad mood | ¿Por qué estás de buen ≠ mal . . . ?
12. I'm sorry | Lo . . . .
13. to make furious | Me da . . . .
14. I can't believe it | Parece . . . / . . . .
15. to see someone again | ¿Cuándo volveremos a . . . ?
16. that's nothing new | Eso no es ninguna . . . .
17. of course not! | ¡Claro que . . . !
18. to need | Me hace . . . mucho dinero.
19. to hurt | ¿Te . . . ?
20. more or less | Cuesta más . . . . . . diez dólares.
21. (what time) is good for you?/(two) is good for me/when is good for you? | ¿A qué hora le . . . bien?/Las dos me . . . bien. /¿Cuándo le . . . bien?
22. to have a drink | ¿Quiere tomar una . . . ?
23. be careful! | ¡Tenga . . . !

171

MODISMOS 2

1. /espero que sí/creo que sí	/I hope so./I think so.
2. echar de menos	I miss you.
3. ¡qué lástima! (or: ¡pena!)	What a pity!
4. darse la mano	In Spain, they shake hands.
5. estar citado (or: hacer una cita)	I made an appointment with my boy friend.
6. tomar el pelo	Don't pull my leg!
7. quedarse un rato	Why don't you stay a while?
8. en cuanto a mí	As for me, I don't agree.
9. tomar el desayuno	We are going to have breakfast.
10. /ponerse de pie /estar de pie	Stand up!/I'm standing up.
11. estar de buen ≠ mal humor	Why are you in a good ≠ bad mood?
12. lo siento	I'm sorry.
13. darse rabia	It makes me furious.
14. parece increíble (or: mentira)	I can't believe it.
15. volver a ver	When will we see you again?
16. no es ninguna novedad	That's nothing new.
17. ¡claro que no!	Of course not!
18. hacer falta	I need a lot of money.
19. ¿te duele? (doler)	Does it hurt?
20. más o menos	It costs more or less ten dollars.
21. /¿(a qué hora) le viene bien?/(las dos) me viene bien/ ¿cuándo le viene bien?	/What time is good for you?/Two is good for me. /When is good for you?
22. tomar una copa	Do you want to have a drink?
23. tener cuidado	Be careful!

IDIOMS 3

1. what's up?	¿Qué . . . ?
2. to agree	Estoy . . . .
3. to put someone out	No quiero . . . ./No me . . . .
4. to realize	No me dí . . . .
5. I'm very grateful don't mention it	Estoy muy . . . . No hay . . . . / De . . . .
6. to worry about someone	Está . . . por su hijo.
7. to have a good time	A . . . bien./Nos . . . mucho.
8. to be successful	La obra tuvo . . . .
9. give me a kiss	¡Dame un . . . !
10. with pleasure!	¿Quiere venir con nosotros? Con . . . .
11. to queue (US: stand in line)	Tiene que hacer . . . para ir al cine.
12. to earn a good living	¿Se gana su . . . ?/¿Gana . . . ?
13. to fall behind, come late	Lleva . . . .
14. to feel like a million bucks ≠ under the weather	Estoy en plena . . . . ≠ No me . . . .
15. to take turns	A cada cual su . . . .
16. what a pain in the neck!	¿Qué . . . !/ . . . !/ . . . !/ . . . !
17. to tell the truth	Para decir la . . . , no me gusta.
18. help yourself	¡S . . . !
19. it's not my cup of tea	No me . . . ./No me . . . .
20. /you gotta be kidding!/Not on your life!	/ ¡Estás . . . ! / ¡No me . . . ! / ¡No me . . . ! / ¡Ni . . . !
21. to get on one's nerves	/Me pone . . . ./Me da . . . .
22. /to look well/to look nice (place)	/Tiene buena . . . ./Este sitio no tiene buen . . . .
23. in the first place	En . . . . . . , no estoy de acuerdo.

173

MODISMOS 3

1. ¿qué pasa?	What's up?
2. estar de acuerdo	I agree.
3. molestar	I don't want to put you out. You're not putting me out.
4. darse cuenta	I don't realize.
5. estoy muy agradecido/no hay de que/de nada	I'm very grateful. Don't mention it.
6. estar preocupado	She worries over (US: for) her son.
7. ¡a pasarlo bien! /divertirse	/Have a good time!/We had a good time.
8. tener éxito	The play was successful.
9. dame un beso	Give me a kiss.
10. con mucho gusto	Do you want to come with us? With pleasure.
11. hacer cola	You must queue to go to the cinema.
12. /ganarse su vida /ganar dinero	/Does he earn a good living?/Does he make money?
13. llevar retraso	/He has fallen behind./He came late.
14. estar en plena forma ≠ no encontrarse bien	I feel like a million bucks./I feel under the weather.
15. a cada cual su turno	We'll take turns.
16. ¡qué pelma! / ¡pesado!/ ¡pelmazo! / ¡latoso!	What a pain in the neck!
17. para decir la verdad	To tell the truth, I don't like her.
18. ¡sírvase!	Help yourself!
19. /no me apetece/me gusta	It's not my cup of tea.
20. / ¡estás bromeando! / ¡de veras!/ ¡no me digas!/ ¡ni hablar!	You gotta be kidding! Not on your life!
21. /ponerse nervioso /dar la lata	She gets on my nerves.
22. /tener buena cara /tener buen aspecto	You look well. This place doesn't look nice.
23. en primer lugar	In the first place, I don't agree.

CONGRATULATIONS!!

You are no longer a beginner.
You can now go on to El Gimmick, the first
uncensored, realistic vocabulary learning book.

KEY

Lección 1, page 1
1) ¿Es una mesa grande? 2) No es una puerta negra. 3) Hasta pronto.
4) ¿Es un perro pequeño? 5) ¡Jolín! 6) No es un libro negro y grande; es
un libro grande y azul. 7) ¿Qué es? Es un reloj. 8) ¿Es un teléfono rojo?
9) No es una silla pequeña. 10) ¡Es un despertador blanco? 11) ¿Es una
pared azul? 12) No es un ratón. 13) ¿Es un lápiz negro? 14) No es un
gato grande.

Lección 1, page 2
1) Sí, es un gato pequeño. No, no es un gato pequeño. 2) Sí, es un perro
blanco. No, no es un perro blanco. 3) Sí, es un teléfono azul. No, no es un
teléfono azul. 4) Sí, es una pared blanca. No, no es una pared blanca. 5) Sí,
es un libro negro. No, no es un libro negro. 6) Sí, es un bolígrafo. No, no es
un bolígrafo. Etc.

Lección 2, page 4
1) ¿Qué tal? ¿Muy bien gracias y tú? 2) ¿Son cigarrillos fuertes? 3) ¿Son
abrigos marrones? 4) Lo siento. Perdona. 5) ¿Son anchas las calles? 6) Es
la hora. 7) Las chicas son jóvenes y delgadas. 8) Eso es. 9) Los chicos son
ricos, pero los niños son pobres. 10) ¿Puede repetirlo por favor?

Lección 2, page 5
1) tíos débiles 2) mujeres pequeñas 3) niños fuertes 4) calcetines marrones
5) abrigos largos 6) ceniceros bonitos 7) mecheros cortos 8) tardes malas
9) relojes viejos 10) niñas grandes, 11) calles estrechas 12) papeles gruesos
13) sombreros azules 14) libros rojos 15) llaves grandes 16) cajas verdes
17) chicos felices 18) cerillas largas 19) lecciones fáciles 20) perros blancos.

Lección 2, page 6
1) No, la mujer no es grande — no, las mujeres no son grandes. 2) No, el
hombre no es débil — no son débiles. 3) No, el libro no es gordo — no son
gordos. 4) No, el cuarto no es pequeño — no son pequeños. 5) No, la
lección no es interesante — no son interesantes. 6) No, la mesa no es liviana
— no son livianas. 7) No, el zapato no es pequeño — no son pequeños. 8) No,
el niño no es gordo — no son gordos. 9) No, la chica no es joven — no son
jóvenes. 10) El zapato no es ancho — no son anchos. Etc.

Lección 2, page 7
1) No, no son relojes azules — no es un reloj azul. 2) No, no son hombres
gordos — no es un hombre gordo. 3) No, no son mujeres felices — no es una

mujer feliz. 4) No, no son cajas amarillas — No es una caja amarilla. 5) No, no son zapatos grandes — no es un zapato grande. 6) No, no son calles estrechas — no es una calle estrecha. 7) No, no son niños bonitos — no es un niño bonito. 8) No, no son impermeables largos — no es un impermeable largo. 9) No, no son sombreros rojos — no es un sombrero rojo. 10) No, no son cuartos viejos — no es un cuarto viejo. 11) No, no son gatos negros — no es un gato negro. 12) No, no son tíos fuertes — no es un tío fuerte. 13) No, no son las últimas lecciones — no es la última lección. 14) No, no son chicos ricos — no es un chico rico. 15) No, no son perros gordos — no es un perro gordo. 16) No, no son zapatos azul marino — no es un zapato azul marino. 17) No, no son cigarrillos malos — no es un cigarrillo. 18) No, no son sombreros verdes — no es un sombrero verde. 19) No, no son llaves pequeñas — no es una llave pequeña. 20) No, no son ratones blancos — no es un ratón blanco.

Lección 2, page 7
1) Es un perro blanco. ¿Es un perro blanco? ¿Son perros blancos? 2) ¿Es una tarde larga? ¿Son tardes largas? 3) ¿Es un mechero viejo? ¿Son mecheros viejos? 4) ¿Es una calle estrecha? ¿Son calles estrechas? 5) ¿Es un libro grueso? ¿Son libros gruesos? 6) ¿Es un cuarto pequeño? ¿Son cuartos pequeños? 7) ¿Es un impermeable amarillo? ¿Son impermeables amarillos? 8) ¿Es la primera lección? ¿Son las primeras lecciones? 9) ¿Es un gato grande? ¿Son gatos grandes? 10) ¿Es un sombrero verde? ¿Son sombreros verdes?

Lección 2, page 8
1) ¿Puede repetir, por favor? 2) El niño joven es malo. 3) No es eso. 4) El cenicero no es verde. 5) Las calles no son anchas. 6) Lo siento. 7) La tía es grande y gorda. 8) Los tíos son pobres pero interesantes. 9) ¡Es la hora! 10) ¡Caramba! 11) ¡Dispense! 12) Buenas tardes. Qué tal? 13) Los libros no son gruesos. 14) La primera lección es larga. 15) La chica es delgada, yo también. 16) El hombre no es gordo, yo tampoco. 17) El mechero es viejo pero bueno. 18) Los niños son fuertes. 19) Es correcto. Eso es. 20) El sombrero es pequeño. 21) El primer cuarto es pequeño. 22) Los zapatos son grandes. 23) La pared es roja y azul. 24) El abrigo es negro pero el sombrero es azul marino. 25) Unos libros son interesantes. 26) La chica rica es joven. 27) El grán teléfono es rojo. 28) Los calcetines amarillos son pequeños.

Lección 3, page 13
1) ¿Es tu (su) pañuelo? No, es suyo. 2) ¿Son sus botas (de él)? No, son suyas (de ella). 3) ¿Qué pasa? 4) ¿De quién es este bolso? 5) No, no son mis cuellos vueltos, son suyos (de ella). 6) Muchas gracias. De nada. 7) ¿Es

tu pantalón demasiado corto? 8) ¿Lo pescas? 9) No son tus corbatas, son suyas. 10) No importa. 11) Qué más? Nada más.

Lección 3, page 13
1) Sus guantes no son bonitos, ni pequeños. 2) Mis deberes no son fáciles. 3) Sus nuevas botas no son grandes. 4) La última lección no es interesante. 5) Sus vestidos no son pequeños. 6) Su bonito y nuevo traje no es negro. 7) Nuestra pizarra no es ancha. 8) Mi pantalón no es corto. 9) Mi cuello vuelto no es liviano. 10) Su bolso no es viejo. 11) Su corbata no es amarilla. 12) Nuestras lecciones no son felices. 13) Sin duda, mis vaqueros no son grandes. 14) Mi mesa no es pesada. 15) Su calle no es estrecha. 16) Su coche no es pequeño. 17) Sus vestidos no son blancos ni azules.

Lección 3, page 14
1) Es la suya. 2) Es la mía. 3) Son los suyos. 4) Es la suya. 5) Es el suyo. 6) Son los vuestros. 7) Es la nuestra. 8) Es el mío. 9) Es el suyo. 10) Es el suyo. 11) Es la nuestra. 12) Es la mía. 13) Es el suyo. 14) Son los vuestros. 15) Son los suyos. 16) Es el suyo. 17) Es el tuyo. 18) Es el suyo. 19) Es la suya. 20) Son las suyas. 21) Es la suya. 22) Son los vuestros. 23) Es el suyo. 24) Son las tuyas. 25) Son las mías 26) Son las tuyas. 27) Son los tuyos. 28) Son las nuestras.

Lección 4, page 16
1) el libro del tío 2) de la 3) de la 4) de los 5) de la 6) del 7) del 8) del 9) de la 10) del 11) de las 12) de los 13) de la 14) del 15) de 16) del 17) del 18) del 19) de los 20) del 21) de los 22) del 23) de la 24) de la 25) de la 26) del 27) del

Lección 4, page 17
1) Son las dos y media. 2) Son las cinco menos cuarto. 3) Son las ocho menos diez. 4) Son las siete. 5) ¿Qué hora es?

Lección 4, page 17
1) Los ojos de Pedro son verdes. 2) ¿Cómo se escribe? 3) La boca de la chica es ancha. 4) La mujer que es alta es rica. 5) ¡Espera un momento! 6) ¿Qué hay de nuevo? Nada importante. 7) La cara de Juanita es fina. 8) Las piernas de la tía son gordas. 9) Por eso es pobre. 10) Los coches de los hombres son grandes. 11) ¿Cuál es su coche? 12) ¿Por qué los jerseyes de las chicas son largos? 13) ¿Cuál es su paraguas? 14) ¿Qué hombre es suyo?

Lección 5, page 21
1) Es inteligente. 2) Es médico. 3) ¿Dónde está Vd.? 4) Las lecciones no son difíciles. 5) Soy americana. 6) Los niños son míos. 6) Eres guapa y

rica. 8) Es abogado. 9) El jefe es feo. 10) El trabajo es difícil. 11) ¿Está cerca de mí? 12) ¿Es Vd. española? 13) ¿Es el tuyo? 14) Estoy cansado. 15) El trabajo es fácil. 16) Es simpático. 17) ¿Por qué está Vd. detrás de la puerta? 18) ¿Quiénes son? 19) El profesor es malo. 20) Son las diez. 21) El gato está en la mesa. 22) El libro está debajo de la silla. 23) ¿Está Vd. en frente de mí? 24) ¿Quién es? 25) Es mío. 26) Estoy enfermo. 27) ¿Dónde está? Está aquí. 28) El hombre es alto.

Lección 5, page 22
1) Es interesante. 2) No es posible. 3) ¿Hace sol? 4) No hace frío. 5) ¿Es verdad? 6) Es demasiado temprano. 7) ¿Es caro? 8) No, es barato. 9) Hace buen tiempo. 10) Es aburrido. 11) Hace calor. 12) Es bonito.

Lección 5, page 23
1) Mi bicicleta es rápida y la tuya también. Mi bicicleta no es rápida y la tuya tampoco. 2) Su hermano es loco y tú también. Su hermano no es loco y tú tampoco. 3) Tu cuarto está sucio y el mío también. Tu cuarto no está sucio y el mío tampoco. 4) El coche de la policía es rápido y el mío también. El coche de la policía no es rápido y el mío tampoco. 5) Su hija es inteligente y la tuya también. Su hija no es inteligente y la tuya tampoco. 6) El invierno es frío y el otoño también. El invierno no es frío y el otoño tampoco. 7) Su botella está vacía y la suya también. Su botella no esta vacía y la suya tampoco. 8) Su profesor es aburrido y tú también. Su profesor no es aburrido y tú tampoco. 9) Su novio es feo y tú también. Su novio no es feo y tú tampoco. 10) Soy fuerte y ella también. No soy fuerte y ella tampoco. 11) La ropa está limpia y el cuarto también. La ropa no está limpia y el cuarto tampoco. 12) El cine está lleno y la calle también. El cine no está lleno y la calle tampoco. 13) Estamos aquí y ellos también. No estamos aquí y ellos tampoco. 14) El gato está debajo de la mesa y el perro también. El gato no está debajo de la mesa y el perro tampoco. 15) Tu sombrero está en la mesa y el suyo también. Tu sombrero no está en la mesa y el suyo tampoco. 16) Mis vaqueros están sucios y los tuyos también. Mis vaqueros no están sucios y los tuyos tampoco. 17) Nuestros cuellos vueltos son bonitos y los suyos también. Nuestros cuellos vueltos no son bonitos y los suyos tampoco. 18) Nuestros niños son difíciles y los suyos también. Nuestros niños no son difíciles y los suyos tampoco. 19) La sopa está fría y yo también. La sopa no está fría y yo tampoco. 20) El barco es rápido y el coche también. El barco no es rápido y el coche tampoco.

Lección 6, page 27
1) ¿Hay treinta horas en un día? 2) ¿Son estas carreteras peligrosas? ¿Cuáles son las peligrosas? 3) ¿Hay taxis en las calles esta tarde? 4) ¿Hay hombres locos en este cuarto? 5) ¿Hay botellas vacías en la mesa? 6) ¿Hay caramelos en la mesa? 7) ¿Hay profesores aburridos en el cuarto? 8) Hay tres coches

bonitos en frente de mi ventana. ¿Cuáles son? 9) Hay una botella llena debajo de la mesa. 10) Hay una lección aburrida en el libro. ¿Cuál?

Lección 6, page 28
1) These bags are on the table. 2) Those suits are small for these men. 3) These clocks are ours and those are yours. 4) That coat is mine and this one is yours. 5) Those guys are far away from Carmen, but her guy is near. 6) Those streets are wide but this one is narrow. 7) These bottles are empty but those are full. 8) That lady is American but these are Spanish. 9) This doctor is mine and that one is yours. 10) This house is ours and that one over there is too. 11) These cars and those over there are pretty. 12) This is good. 13) This work is very boring. 14) That guy is crazy and those over there are also.

Lección 6, page 28
1) Está tía es loca pero interesante. 2) ¿Es ese tío aburrido? Éste no. 3) Ese coche es grande, pero éstos no. 4) ¿Cuál es tu niño? Éste. 5) ¿Es tuya aquella casa? 6) No, pero ésta es mía. 7) Estos médicos son españoles y ésos son americanos. 8) Estos libros son de Carmen y aquéllos son míos. 9) Aquel abrigo es mío y éste también. 10) Esos niños son guapos y éste también. 11) Este zapato y aquél son míos. 12) ¿Son estas sillas tuyas? No, pero ésta es mía. 13) Esos profesores son simpáticos y éstos también. 14) Aquel abogado es mío. ¿Es éste el suyo?

Lección 7, page 33
1) I have known Carmen for two years. 2) He always wants the same thing. 3) Perhaps we can go now. 4) He sometimes comes back very late. 5) I'm used to eating a lot. 6) This thing costs at least two dollars. 7) It rains above all in the autumn (fall). 8) Can you bring a coffee to Peter? 9) We've been here for five years. 10) The cops are used to being tough. 11) Can we do this work? 12) He's been reading this book for a week. 13) I am in a hurry to buy this car. 14) Every day I take a nap in the afternoon.

Lección 7, page 33
1) ¿Entiendes generalmente al profesor? 2) Supongo que conoces la respuesta. 3) ¿Tengo razón? 4) Hace buen tiempo hoy. 5) Hace dos años que es médico. 6) ¿Conoces bien al profesor? 7) ¿De quién es? Es suyo. 8) ¿Puedes venir esta tarde? 9) ¿Es tuya esta cosa? 10) No es médico, tampoco es abogado. 11) ¿Quieres ir con ese tío loco? 12) No, quiero ir de paseo con Pablo. 13) ¿Conoces a Carmen desde el verano? 14) No suelo llegar a tiempo.

Lección 7, page 34
1) I only want to drink a beer. 2) The boss has only one car. 3) I eat with

no one. 4) He never comes back late. 5) I can't do this work yet. 6) I
don't want anything. 7) This man only drinks wine. 8) He is never right.

Lección 7, page 34
1) ¿Sueles beber mucho? 2) No veo a nadie. 3) Su novio no come nunca en
casa. 4) No queremos más que uno. 5) No hace buen tiempo todavía. 6)
No leo más que un libro este mes. 7) No puede hace nada. 8) No llueve
nunca en verano en Madrid.

Lección 7, page 35
1) I always smoke after eating. 2) The kids never play in class. 3) He
usually works until six in the afternoon. 4) You never remember my name.
5) I dream at least every night. 6) I think it's cold. 7) Why have you been
talking for an hour? 8) Do you often meet interesting men? 9) We rarely
study on Saturdays. 10) I've been here for a year. 11) He gives me English
lessons every day. 12) You always ask too many questions. 13) She never
leaves the kids alone. 14) I often answer quickly.

Lección 7, page 35
1) Hace una hora que jugamos. 2) ¿Cuánto cuestan los libros? 3) ¿Qué te
parece? 4) Habla desde hace dos horas. 5) Por fin empiezo este trabajo.
6) Los dos empiezan el trabajo a las seis de la mañana. 7) ¿Quién habla?
8) ¿Está hablando con tu jefe? 9) Dejamos de trabajar ahora. 10) Estoy
aprendiendo español desde hace un año. 11) Estoy hablando a los niños.
12) Estamos aquí desde hace cinco años. 13) Apenas nieva en Madrid.
14) Llevamos generalmente abrigos y botas en invierno.

Lección 8, page 39
1) We never have enough time. 2) He has only two sons. 3) There's no one
in the room. 4) They're not here yet. 5) He only speaks Spanish. 6) He
gives nothing to his wife. 7) I don't speak to anyone.

Lección 8, page 39
1) No pienso en nada. 2) No está nunca con Vd. 3) No tengo más que un
niño. No tengo sino un niño. 4) No está aquí todavía. 5) No encuentra
nunca a nadie de vacaciones. 6) No juega más que por la noche con los
niños. No juega sino por la noche con los niños. 7) No tengo nada.

Lección 9, page 43
1) El profesor no tiene siempre razón. 2) ¿Tiene Vd. tiempo esta tarde?
3) ¿Cuántos cigarrillos tiene? 4) Ese hombre de negocios siempre tiene éxito.
5) No tengo hambre, tengo sed. 6) ¿Tiene algunos bocadillos? Sí, tenemos
algunos. 7) De todas formas, tengo miedo. 8) Casi tiene razón. 9) Nunca
tenemos dinero. 10) No tiene más que dos dólares. ¿Tiene Vd. algunos?

11) No tengo más suerte. 12) Tienen quince años juntos. 13) Tengo a menudo frío en invierno y calor en verano. 14) Rara vez tiene sueño. 15) La secretaria del jefe no se equivoca nunca. 16) Solemos beber mucha cerveza una vez por semana. 17) Siempre bebe cerveza en el restaurante. 18) Tenemos prisa, por otra parte, quiero una comida buena.

Lección 9, page 44
1) Tenemos que comer rápidamente. 2) No hay que hablar con ella sola. 3) Debe ser puntual cada día. 4) Tiene que aprender rápidamente. 5) Es necesario comer para vivir. 6) Hay que descansar de vez en cuando. 7) Tengo que ir ahora. 8) No tienes que decírmelo si no quieres.

Lección 9, page 44
1) We always have to wait for Carmen. 2) We must eat instead of speaking. 3) You must not be late. 4) I have to go now. 5) It's necessary to work in life. 6) Must you come back now? 7) I must say something to you. 8) We must go out later.

Lección 10, page 48
1) I sleep from time to time in the afternoon. 2) All in all he goes out often. 3) He never comes. 4) I don't say anything to anyone. 5) I asked for a black coffee instead of a white coffee. 6) I don't feel it any more. 7) I prefer wine, do you? 8) I don't like Paul any more, but he still comes every day. 9) I'm writing the letter although I don't have much time. 10) The teacher never repeats the lesson. 11) They don't talk about Madrid any more. 12) They have been living in New York for two years now. 13) The students are still repeating the lesson. 14) The children are not sleeping yet. 15) Before going out we have to pay the bill. 16) We all die one day. 17) This time suits the teacher. 18) We're going on working in spite of the rain.

Lección 11, page 54
1) No me gusta este pastel duro y no lo quiero. 2) No puedo verles con el jefe. 3) No puedo escucharle. 4) No se lo mando. 5) El profesor es aburrido y a menudo no les escuchamos. 6) ¿Hace cuánto tiempo que no la ve? 7) Tiene que ir arriba para encontrarlo. 8) Esta muñeca es cara pero me gusta mucho. 9) Juego a un juego maravilloso. ¿Lo conoce Vd.? 10) Es una chica fenomenal. ¿La conoce Vd.? 11) Las lecciones son demasiado difíciles y no las entendemos. 12) Necesito unos cigarrillos y tengo que comprarlos. 13) Conozco a esta mujer aunque no me gusta. 14) ¿Les ve? 15) ¿Lo quiere Vd. para el lunes? 16) Lleva vestidos viejos y le gustan. 17) Viven en los cuartos de arriba. 18) No tenemos más que dos comidas al día. 19) Los estudiantes desilusionan a menudo al profesor pero éste les quiere. 20) Tomo el metro. ¿Lo toma Vd.? 21) No le gustan más que los bolsos caros; aunque no los compra nunca. 22) Pegas a tu mujer de vez en cuando? No,

no le pego nunca. 23) Estoy comprando una casa pero a mi novio no le gusta. 24) La lección empieza. ¿La encuentras difícil? 25) La palabra es difícil. No puedo escribirla. 26) El trabajo es más bien largo. No quiero hacerlo. 27) El libro es difícil pero tengo que acabarlo. 28) A mí me gustan las zanahorias. ¿Le gustan a Vd.? 29) Le odio aunque estás loco por él. 30) Conozco muchas cosas interesantes. ¿Las conoce Vd.?

Lección 11, page 53
1) la 2) ella 3) las 4) de él 5) lo 6) le 7) la 8) lo 9) lo 10) las 11) verle 12) nos 13) los 14) le 15) lo 16) la 17) los 18) lo 19) lo 20) la 21) lo 22) la 23) los 24) la 25) los 26) lo 27) la 28) les

Lección 12, page 59
1) Conozco a su madre. ¿La conoce Vd.? 2) Afortunadamente, la criada hace el trabajo de la casa. 3) Les dice todos sus problemas. 4) Le da un suéter bonito. ¿Que le das tú? 5) Piensa a menudo en su mujer. 6) Hace mucho tiempo que trabajo. ¿Trabaja Vd. todavía? 7) ¿Le habla a menudo? No le hablo casi nunca. 8) Es tonto, pero a pesar de eso me gusta. 9) Intento entenderle. 10) Le quiero y me quiere. 11) Le espero desde hace dos horas. 12) ¿Qué trae de comer para sus familiares? 13) ¿Tienes ganas de enseñarme tu trabajo? 14) Hace una hora que escuchamos a ese hombre extraño. 15) No podemos verles esta noche. 16) Sus abuelos y su mujer le dan un traje nuevo. 17) No quiero decirles que es loco. 18) No me gusta el café, sin embargo suelo beberlo. 19) No tiene que decirnos sus problemas. 20) Anda, te escucho. 21) ¿Desde hace cuánto tiempo está Vd. enseñándoles español? 22) Sus suegros te esperan desde hace una hora. 23) No quiero dárselo. 24) Trata de llevárselo. 25) Esa chica mona vuelve a llamarle. 26) A pesar del tiempo, nos invitan. 27) incluso a mí, me gustan mucho los hombres, sobre todo el mío. 28) No hay que llamarles ahora.

Lección 13, page 62
1) ¿Nunca se pasea Vd. por la mañana? No, no me paseo nunca por la mañana. 2) No voy nunca al cine los domingos. 3) ¿Tiene suerte alguna vez? No, nunca tengo suerte. 4) No entendemos nunca al profesor.

Lección 13, page 62
1) ¿Conoce Vd. Madrid? 2) ¿Sabes conducir? 3) ¿Conoce ella a su mujer? 4) No conozco la respuesta. 5) ¿Conoce a su familia? 6) ¿Sabe nadar? 7) ¿Sabe Vd. español? 8) ¿Conoces este restaurante? 9) Conoce ella a su familia? 10) ¿Sabes éso?

Lección 13, page 63
1) Sé que tiene Vd. razón. 2) Pienso que es un tío simpático. 3) ¿A quién mira Vd.? 4) Pienso que tiene éxito. 5) Sé que necesita dinero. 6) ¿Qué es?

7) ¿Quién es? 8) ¿Quiénes son aquellas mujeres? 9) ¿Quién es ella? 10)
¿Quiénes son esos hombres? 11) ¿A quién habla Vd.? 12) Piensa que me
equivoco. 13) Piensa que Vd. tiene suerte. 14) ¿Qué busca Vd.? 15) ¿Quién
me busca? 16) ¿Qué bebe Vd.? 17) No piensan que entiendes. 18) Estoy
de acuerdo con que debe hacerlo. 19) No sé qué decirle. 20) El piso me
parece demasiado pequeño. 21) ¿Qué piso? 22) ¿Qué coche quiere Vd.?
23) ¿Qué clase de carne quiere? 24) No sé quien es. 25) Veo a las mujeres
que están en la calle. 26) Sabe a quien quiero. 27) ¿Qué perro es el de Vd.?
28) No tiene que decirme que me equivoco.

Lección 14, page 67
1) ¿Están tus padres de viaje ahora? 2) De momento, trabajo media jornada.
Está comiendo todavía. Hace dos horas que está comiendo. 4) ¿La carta?
Estoy escribiéndola ahora. 5) Los niños juegan. 6) Duermen todos arriba.
7) Lleva el mismo abrigo que el mío. 8) Me enseña español y aprendo.
9) Vamos a un sitio bonito. 10) Lo bebo ahora. 11) Está llamándole.
12) Le espero. 13) Nos escuchan. 14) ¿Vuelven ahora? 15) Está lloviendo
y nevando al mismo tiempo. 16) Empiezo el trabajo esta semana. 17) ¿Qué
están haciendo? Están andando. 18) Se ríen de mí. 19) Cierro la ventana.
20) Está diciéndoselo. 21) Se lo doy. 22) Nos invitan esta noche. 23) Está
explicándonos el problema. 24) Estoy haciéndolo ahora.

Lección 15, page 72
1) I've been studying Spanish for five years. 2) For how long have you loved
him? 3) According to him, they have been here since the summer. 4) You've
been working since this morning. 5) How long have you been married?
6) We've been working together for two months. 7) We've been building our
house since autumn. 8) He's been waiting for you for an hour. 9) He's been
writing to her for a long time. 10) They've been living together since last
spring. 11) Have they been here for two hours? 12) I've been listening to
you for ten minutes. 13) I've been trying to help him since last year. 14) I've
known them for ten years.

Lección 15, page 72
1) ¿Hace cuánto tiempo que estás aquí? 2) Estamos comiendo desde hace
una hora. 3) Viven en su nueva casa desde el verano. 4) ¿Hace cuánto
tiempo que trabajas aquí? 5) Hace una hora que andamos. 6) Está casado
con ella desde el verano. 7) ¿Hace cuánto tiempo que está enfermo? 8) Hace
un año que estoy divorciada. 9) Trato de entenderle desde el principio.
10) Hace cinco años que tengo que trabajar con él. 11) ¿Hace cuánto tiempo
que vivís juntos? 12) ¿El libro? Estoy escribiéndolo desde hace un año.
13) ¿Hace cuánto tiempo que la conoces? 14) Trato de vender mi coche
desde hace seis meses.

Lección 16, page 76

1) She will see her boyfriend next week? 2) Do you know whether he will help us in any case? 3) We will stop working in an hour. 4) We'll be hungry soon. 5) I don't know whether he'll come with us. 6) He says he won't buy another car like that. 7) They don't know either whether they will be able to do it or not. 8) This thing will cost a lot of money in a few years. 9) Will he tell you tomorrow? 10) Will he travel next summer? 11) Will you go out this evening? 12) We'll have to tell him tomorrow. 13) I'll wear my new suit tonight. 14) Will you call me in an hour?

Lección 16, page 76

1) Estaré en casa esta tarde. 2) ¿Necesitarás más dinero? 3) Te llamaré esta noche de todas formas. 4) Iremos de paseo a pesar del mal tiempo. 5) ¿Su carta? La contestaré mañana. 6) Podré hacerlo la semana próxima. 7) Tendrás que preguntarle esta noche. 8) Beberá mucho vino esta noche. 9) Tendrás un catarro por la lluvia. 10) Estaré listo a las diez. 11) Le hará falta una píldora para su dolor de cabeza. 12) Estoy segura de que tendrá suerte. 13) Se acostumbrará Vd. pronto. 14) Le llevaré conmigo esta tarde.

Lección 17, page 79

1) If you are tired, will you go to bed? Sí, si estoy cansado, iré a la cama. 2) If your throat hurts, will you take a pill? Sí, si me duele la garganta, tomaré un comprimido. 3) If you have a cold, will you be tired? Sí, si tengo un catarro estaré cansada. 4) If you ask me something, will I answer you? Sí, si me pregunta Vd. algo, le contestaré. 5) If you can do it yourself, will you do it? Sí, si puedo hacerlo sola, lo haré. 6) If you call me up, will I answer you? Sí, si me llamas, te contestaré. 7) If a friend has to go to the doctor, will I go with him? Sí, si un amigo tiene que ir al médico, iré con él. 8) If I am hungry, will you give me something to eat? Sí, si tienes hambre, te daré algo de comer. 9) If it's nice out, will we go to the movies? Sí, si hace buen tiempo, iremos al cine. 10) If you have the money, will you buy a new house? Sí, si tengo dinero, compraré una casa nueva.

Lección 17, page 79

1) ¿Si necesita Vd. ayuda, me llamará? No, si necesito ayuda, no le llamaré. 2) ¿Si adelgazan, se sentirán mejor? No, si adelgazan, no se sentirán mejor. 3) ¿Si tiene mucho dinero, comprará un nuevo piso? No, si tiene mucho dinero, no comprará un nuevo piso. 4) ¿Si estoy malo, vendrás conmigo al médico? No, si estás malo, no vendré contigo al médico. 5) ¿Si tengo que ir de viaje la semana próxima, vendrás conmigo? No, si tienes que ir de viaje la semana próxima, no vendré contigo. 6) ¿Si tiene suerte, ganará mucho dinero? No, si tiene suerte, no ganará mucho dinero. 7) ¿Si tu mujer me quiere, estarás feliz? No, si mi mujer te quiere, no estaré feliz. 8) ¿Si no comprenden, les ayudará el profesor? No, si no comprenden, el profesor no

les ayudará. 9) ¿Si no puedes hacerlo, me lo dirás? No, si no puedo hacerlo, no te lo diré. 10) ¿Si el jefe se equivoca, lo sabremos? No, si el jefe se equivoca, no lo sabremos. 11) ¿Si no estás acostumbrado a beber, estarás enfermo? No, si no estoy acostumbrado a beber, no estaré enfermo. 12) ¿Si el restaurante es caro, iremos de todas formas? No, si el restaurante es caro, no iremos.

Lección 18, page 82
1) largo, más largo que, menos largo que, el/la más largo(a), tan largo como
2) malo, peor que, el/la peor, tan malo como 3) dulce, más dulce que, menos dulce que, el/la más dulce, tan dulce como 4) caluroso, más caluroso que, menos caluroso que, el/la más caluroso(a), tan caluroso como 5) fino, más fino que, menos fino que, el/la más fino(a), tan fino como 6) fuerte, más fuerte que, menos fuerte que, el/la más fuerte, tan fuerte como 7) serio, más serio que, menos serio que, el/la más serio(a), tan serio como 8) justo, más justo que, menos justo que, el/la más justo(a), tan justo como 9) guapo, más guapo que, menos guapo que, el/la más guapo(a), tan guapo como 10) desordenado, más desordenado que, menos desordenado que, el/la más desordenado(a), tan desordenado como 11) seguro, más seguro que, menos seguro que, el/la más seguro(a), tan seguro como 12) lejano, más lejano que, menos lejano que, el/la más lejano(a), tan lejano como 13) infeliz, más infeliz que, menos infeliz que, el/la más infeliz, tan infeliz como 14) pesado, más pesado que, menos pesado que, el/la más pesado(a), tan pesado como 15) barato, más barato que, menos barato que, el/la más barato(a), tan barato como 16) inteligente, más inteligente que, menos inteligente que, el/la más inteligente, tan inteligente como 17) caro, más caro que, menos caro que, el/la más caro(a), tan caro como 18) viejo, más viejo que, menos viejo que, el/la más viejo(a), tan viejo como 19) loco, más loco que, menos loco que, el/la más loco(a), tan loco como 20) lleno, más lleno que, menos lleno que, el/la más lleno, tan lleno como 21) profundo, más profundo que, menos profundo que, el/la más profundo(a), tan profundo como 22) débil, más débil que, menos débil que, el/la más débil, tan débil como 23) bonito, más bonito que, menos bonito que, el/la más bonito(a), tan bonito como 24) peligroso, más peligroso que, menos peligroso que, el/la más peligroso(a), tan peligroso como 25) interesante, más interesante que, menos interesante, el/la más interesante, tan interesante como 26) aburrido, más aburrido que, menos aburrido que, el/la más aburrido(a), tan aburrido como 27) cortés, más cortés que, menos cortés que, el/la más cortés, tan cortés como 28) bueno, mejor que, el/la mejor, tan bueno como 29) tonto, más tonto que, menos tonto que, el/la más tonto(a), tan tonto como 30) lleno, más lleno que, menos lleno que, el/la más lleno(a), tan lleno como

Leccion 18, page 83
1) la mayor 2) el mejor 3) el más bonito 4) el más limpio 5) la más pobre 6) la más bonita 7) las más difíciles 8) el más caro 9) más precioso 10) la

más maravillosa 11) el más cercano 12) la mayor 13) el mejor 14) el peor

Lección 18, page 83
1) tan seria como 2) tan bonita como 3) tan limpio como 4) tan cerca como
5) tan cara como 6) tan fea como 7) tan mala como 8) tan simpática como
9) tan interesante como 10) tan guapo como 11) tan buena como 12) tan
aburrido como 13) tan graciosa como 14) tan importante como

Lección 18, page 84
1) Es tan guapa como tu hermana. Es más guapa que tu hermana. 2) Nuestro
viaje es tan interesante como el suyo. — es más interesante que — 3) Mis
zapatos son tan baratos como los suyos. — más baratos que — 4) Tus joyas
son tan bonitas como las suyas. — más bonitas que — 5) Este libro es tan
feucho como ése. — más feucho que — 6) Tu pasatiempo es tan aburrido
como el mío. — es más aburrido que — 7) El director es tan malo como su
obra de teatro. — peor que — 8) Esta clase es tan fácil como la última. —
más fácil que — 9) Tu monedero está tan lleno como el mío. — está más
lleno que — 10) Esta novela es tan horrible como la última. — más horrible
que — 11) Esa obra de teatro es tan buena como el libro. — mejor que —
12) Mi ducha está tan caliente como la de Juanita. — más caliente que —
13) Mi dinero es tan bueno como el tuyo. — mejor que — 14) Sus deberes
son tan difíciles como los nuestros. — más difíciles que — 15) Su cuñada es
tan mona como su madre. — más mona que — 16) Mi traje de baño es tan
bonito como el de mi prima. — más bonito que — 17) Su restaurante está
tan lleno como el otro. — más lleno que. 18) Mi cuarto está tan desordenado
como el suyo. — más desordenado que — 19) Mi vestido es tan encantador
como el tuyo. — más encantador que — 20) Es tan perezoso como su padre.
— más perezoso que — 21) Son tan ricos como sus padres. — más ricos que —
22) Estoy tan pobre como Vd. — más pobre que — 23) Los profesores son
tan tontos como los estudiantes. — más tontos que — 24) Su piso es tan alto
como mi casa. — más alto que — 25) Mis compañeros son tan graciosos como
los tuyos. — más graciosos que — 26) Estas montañas son tan altas como un
rascacielos. — más altas que —

Lección 18, page 85
1) triste, tristemente 2) difícil, difícilmente 3) bueno, bien 4) malo, mal
5) serio, seriamente 6) facil, fácilmente 7) lento, lentament 8) largo,
largamente 9) frecuente, frecuentemente 10) dulce, dulcemente 11)
profundo, profundamente 12) rápido, rapidamente 13) gracioso, graciosa-
mente 14) feliz, felizmente 15) seco, secamente 16) raro, raramente 17)
tonto, tontamente 18) inteligente, inteligentemente 19) súbito, súbitamente
20) loco, locamente 21) inmediato, inmediatamente 22) alegre, alegremente
23) maravilloso, maravillosamente

Lección 18, page 86

1) ¿Tiene Vd. algo que hacer esta noche? No, no tengo nada que hacer — 2) ¿Va a alguna parte después de la lección? No, no voy a ninguna parte — 3) ¿Hay alguien importante en el cuarto? No, no hay nadie importante — 4) ¿Irá a cualquier parte conmigo? No, no iré a ninguna parte — 5) ¿Me dará algo de beber? No, no te dará nada — 6) ¿Verán algo interesante en el cine? No, no verán nada — 7) ¿Puede hallar algo divertido que hacer esta noche? No, no puedo hallar nada divertido — 8) ¿Hay aquí alguna tía sexy? No, no hay ninguna tía sexy. 9) ¿Hay algo peor que un policía malo? No hay nada peor que un policía malo. 10) ¿Harás algo interesante esta tarde? No, no haré nada interesante — 11) ¿Alguien viene a verle después de la clase? No, no viene nadie — 12) ¿Va Vd. a alguna parte solo? No, no voy a ninguna parte — 13) ¿Es alguien rico aquí? No, nadie es rico aquí. 14) ¿Vas a verle en alguna parte en Nueva York? No, no a verle en ninguna parte —

Lección 19, page 90

1) ¿Salió de su oficina a las diez? No, no salió de su oficina — 2) ¿Fueron lejos de paseo el domingo pasado? No, no fueron lejos de paseo — 3) ¿Cogió un catarro en la nieve? No, no cogió — 4) ¿Estornudaste hace un momento? No, no estornudé — 5) ¿Te dolieron los dientes la semana pasada? No, no me dolieron los dientes — 6) ¿Occurió eso ayer? No, eso no ocurrió ayer. 7) ¿Tuviste dolor de garganta hace dos semanas? No, no tuve dolor de garganta — 8) ¿Descansó después de su trabajo ayer? No, no descansó — 9) ¿Trajiste los libros sola? No, no traje los libros — 10) ¿Tuvo éxito la obra la semana pasada? No, no tuvo éxito — 11) ¿Tuvo suerte con Vd.? No, no tuvo suerte — 12) ¿Tuviste que ir ayer? No, no tuve que ir — 13) ¿Tuviste miedo de los perros? No, no tuve miedo de los perros. 14) ¿Fueron Vds. veinticinco el mes pasado? No, no fuimos veinticinco — 15) ¿Viviste allí mucho tiempo? No, no viví allí — 16) ¿Te gustó su boda hace un mes? No, no me gustó su boda — 17) ¿Despegó a tiempo el avión? No, el avión no despegó — 18) ¿Lo hiciste con tu marido la semana pasada? No, no lo hice con — 19) ¿Trajo su nuevo abrigo ayer? No, no trajo su nuevo — 20) ¿Te dijeron lo que sabían hace dos dias? No, no me dijeron — 21) ¿Acabaron su lección anoche? No, no acabaron — 22) ¿Oiste lo que dijo? No, no oí lo — 23) ¿Creiste que fué con ella? No, no creí — 24) ¿Compró esa falda en esa tienda el otro día? No, no compró — 25) ¿Tuvimos que salir anoche? No, no tuvimos que — 26) ¿Tuvo que salir tan temprano? No, no tuvo que salir — 27) ¿Te mandaron los libros a tiempo? No, no me mandaron — 28) ¿Odiaste a tus padres cuando se divorciaron? No, no odié a —

Lección 19, page 91

1) hacer, hice, hicimos 2) volver, volví, volvimos 3) recordar, recordé, recordamos 4) alcanzar, alcancé, alcanzamos 5) venir, vine, vinimos 6) cocer, cocí, cocimos 7) oler, olí, olimos 8) ser, fuí, fuimos / estar, estuve,

estuvimos 9) dormir, dormí, dormimos 10) preguntar, pregunté, preguntamos 11) tener, tuve, tuvimos / haber, hubo, hubimos 12) seguir, seguí, seguimos 13) jugar, jugué, jugamos 14) escapar, escapé, escapamos 15) nacer, nací, nacimos 16) conocer, conocí, conocimos / saber, supe, supimos 17) pensar, pensé, pensamos 18) tener costumbre de, tuve — , tuvimos — 19) conducir, conduje, condujimos 20) ir, fuí, fuimos 21) decir, dije, dijimos 22) contar, conté, contamos 23) dar, dí, dimos 24) traer, traje, trajimos 25) ver, ví, vimos 26) elegir, elegí, elegimos 27) oír, oí, oimos 28) llover, llovió 29) leer, leí, leimos 30) entender, entendí, entendimos 31) andar, anduve, anduvimos 32) sugerir, sugerí, sugerimos 33) prometer, prometí, prometimos 34) querer, quise, quisimos 35) empezar, empecé, empezamos 36) querer a, quise a, quisimos a 37) servir, serví, servimos 38) volver, volví, volvimos 39) parecer, parecí, parecimos 40) reconocer, reconocí, reconocimos 41) mover, moví, movimos 42) despertar, desperté, despertamos 43) caer, caí, caimos 44) discutir, discutí, discutimos 45) valer, valí, valimos 46) morir, morí, morimos 47) sentir, sentí, sentimos 48) reir, reí, reimos 49) preferir, preferí, preferimos 50) concluir, concluí, concluimos

Lección 20, page 98

1) What were you doing yesterday while I was sleeping? 2) I was eating when you came. 3) He was answering the question while the others were listening. 4) He was coming to see me when the accident happened. 5) I was buying a new car when I met this guy. 6) The children were watching television while their parents were eating. 7) She was earning their living while he was sleeping. 8) We were drinking while we were working. 9) When you called me, I was taking my bath. 10) When you came in the kitchen, the cat was afraid. 11) We were taking a trip when she got sick. 12) There were a lot of other people in the house when they came in. 13) While she was dying, her husband was with another woman. 14) I was born when my father was abroad.

Lección 20, page 98

1) ¿Que hacías cuando llamé? 2) ¿Por qué trabajaba mientras dormía? 3) Pasaba un examen mientras miraba la tele. 4) La criada limpiaba la casa cuando volvimos. 5) Conducía cuando ocurrió el accidente. 6) Se casaba mientras su hermana se divorciaba. 7) Los estudiantes hacían progresos cuando el profesor tuvo que dejarles. 8) ¿Qué hacíais mientras comíamos? 9) Ganaba mientras perdía. 10) ¿Dormías cuando llamé? 11) ¿Escribían cartas mientras jugábamos? 12) Mientras vivíamos en Nueva York, vimos muchas películas. 13) El avión despegaba cuando lo vimos. 14) Los niños chillaban cuando el padre llegó.

Lección 20, page 99

1) — vino — cenaba. 2) Escribía — llamaste. 3) Comía — trabajaba. 4) Estaba cansada — llegaste. 5) Dejó de leer — entró. 6) Leía — llamó. 7) Ví — entré —. 8) Hablaba — llegó. 9) Andaba — encontré. 10) — volvió — trabajaba. 11) — hablaban — entró —. 12) — vino — comíamos. 13) — salí, llovía. 14) — ví, — reconocí. 15) Acababa — debió —. 16) Soñaba — trabajaba. 17) — ví —, estaba —. 18) Estabas triste — encontré —. 19) — sabía — ví. 20) Estaba decidiendo — decidió —. 21) — empecé —, comenzó — llovió —. 22) Estaba hablando — hizo —. 23) — llegó — salí. 24) Estaba leyendo — miraba —. 25) Vino — comía. 26) Pregunté — dió —. 27) ¿ — reiste — dije — ? 28) Estabas durmiendo — llamé.

Lección 21, page 103

1) Dijo que haría sus maletas. 2) Pensé que tendría miedo. 3) Supimos que haríamos progresos. 4) Supieron que serían capaces de hacerlo. 5) Supo que le buscaría. 6) Le dije que saldría. 7) Escribió que vendría la semana próxima. 8) Tomó el tren que llegaría a tiempo. 9) Pensé que estaría harto pronto. 10) Mi madre supo que conseguiría el divorcio. 11) ¿Pensaste que se enfadaría? 12) Te dije que no tendrías que venir. 13) Dijo que haría muchas faltas por que no es bueno. 14) ¿Creiste que tendría miedo?

Lección 21, page 103

1) No sé si viene. 2) Pensamos que tomaremos el —. 3) Sé que le gustará — 4) Pienso que no estaré —. 5) Decido que iremos —. 6) Dicen que no quieren —. 7) El jefe piensa que — tendrán —. 8) — piensa que su libro será —. 9) Sabemos que llegaremos —. 10) Dice que estará —. 11) Escribe que no vendrá —. 12) Sueño que iré —. 13) Me pregunto si vendrán —. 14) Planea que terminará —.

Lección 21, page 104

1) Me dijo que le gustaría media jornada. Me dice que le gustará trabajar — 2) Supe que nos ayudaría. Sé que nos ayudará. 3) Pensé que mis niños le fastidiarían mucho. Pienso que — le fastidiarán mucho. 4) Estuvo convencido de que estaría harto ya. Está convencido — está —. 5) Pensó que parecía fea. Piensa que parece fea. 6) Supe que no estaría satisfecho. Sé que no estará satisfecho. 7) Creí que tendría razón. Creo que tendrá razón. 8) Nos pareció que no sería tan importante. Nos parece que no será tan importante. 9) Dijo que estaría de acuerdo contigo. Dice que estará —. 10) Pensamos que podrías venir. Pensamos que podrás venir. 11) Pareció que tendría que buscar otro trabajo. Parece que tendrá que —. 12) No supe que estarías tan enferma. No sé si estarás tan enferma. 13) ¿No supiste que te ayudaría? ¿No sabes que te ayudaré? 14) ¿Pensaste que tendría razón? ¿Piensas que tendré razón?

Lección 21, page 104

1) No puede imaginar que su marido es un canalla. No pudo imaginar que su marido era — . 2) Sé que tendrá Vd. suerte. Supe que tendría — . 3) Quiero saber lo que necesitarás. Quise saber lo que necesitarías. 4) Piensa que será capaz de ir. Pensó que sería capaz — . 5) No entendemos lo que nos dice. No entendimos lo que nos dijo. 6) ¿No ves que estaré harta pronto? ¿No viste que estaría harta pronto? 7) Estoy convencida de que necesitará ayuda. Estuve convencida — necesitaría — . 8) No pienso que le gustará esa decisión. No pensé que le gustaría esa — . 9) Sé que no podrás hacerlo. Supe que no podrías — . 10) Pensamos que estará de acuerdo. Pensamos que estaría de — . 11) Pienso que tendremos que ir ahora. Pensé que tendríamos — . 12) Pienso que tendré que ayudarle. Pensé que tendría que — . 13) Pasa que no sabes lo que dices. Pasó que no supiste de lo que decías. 14) Dice que tendrá que trabajar mucho. Dijo que tendría que — .

Lección 22, page 107

1) If you had money, would you buy a new flat? ¿Si tienes dinero, comprarás — ? 2) If you could, would you help me? ¿Si puede, me ayudará? 3) If he came to see you, would you be happy? ¿Si viene a verte, serás feliz? 4) If the tourists had time, they would go to see the museums. Si los turistas tienen tiempo, irán a ver los museos. 5) If the firm was successful, the manager would be glad. Si la companía tiene éxito, el director estará contento. 6) If you didn't understand me, would you tell me? ¿Si no entiende me lo dirá? 7) If it rained, we would take an umbrella. Si llueve, tomaremos un paragüas. 8) If we had to do it, we would do it. Si tenemos que hacerlo, lo haremos. 9) If the weather were bad, we wouldn't go for a walk. Si hace mal tiempo, no iremos de paseo. 10) If we were hungry, we would finish the meat from yesterday. Si tenemos hambre, acabaremos la carne de ayer. 11) If you could come, would you come alone? ¿Si puedes venir, vendrás solo? 12) If he owed you money, he would pay you immediately. Si te debe dinero, te lo pagará inmediatamente. 13) If you wanted, I would give it you. Si quieres te lo daré. 14) If I were in a mess, would you help me? ¿Si estoy en un apuro, me ayudarás?

Lección 22, page 108

1) Sí, si estoy enfermo, iré al médico. Sí, si estuviera — iría — . 2) Sí, si no puedes hacerlo, te ayudaré. Sí, si no pudieras — te ayudaría. 3) Sí, si no tienes bastante dinero, te prestaré un poco. Sí, si no tuvieras — te prestaría — . 4) Sí, si hace buen tiempo, irán a la playa. Sí, si hiciera — irían — . 5) Sí, si tiene tiempo, vendrá con nosotros. Sí, si tuviera — vendría — . 6) Sí, si voy a España, encontraré a tíos interesantes. Sí, si fuera — encontraría — . 7) Sí, si llegas tarde, me enfadaré. Sí, si tuvieras — me enfadaría. 8) Sí, si trabajamos mucho, ganaremos mucho dinero. Sí, si trabajaramos — ganaríamos — . 9) Sí, si recibo amigos esta noche, te invitaré. Sí, si recibiera — te invitaría. 10) Sí, si llueve, nos iremos de todas formas.

Sí, si lloviera — iríamos — . 11) Sí, si estoy mejor, tendré que ir al médico.
Sí, si estuviera mejor, tendría — . 12) Sí, si estoy harta, la dejaré. Sí, si
estuviera harta, la dejaría. 13) Sí, si tengo un catarro, estornudaré mucho.
Sí, si tuviera un catarro, estornudaría mucho. 14) Sí, si su libro fracasa,
estará muy desilusionado. Sí, — fracasara, — estaría — . 15) Sí, si te presto
dinero, me lo devolverás. Sí, si te prestara — me lo devolverías. 16) Sí, si voy
de viaje podrás venir conmigo. Sí, si fuera — podrías — . 17) Sí, si tienes que
ir al médico, iré contigo. Sí, si tuvieras — iría — . 18) Sí, si no sabe que su
amigo está enfermo, se lo diría. Sí, si no supiera — se lo diría. 19) Sí, si
hacemos muchos progresos, estaremos felices. Sí, si hiciéramos — estaríamos
— . 20) Sí, si pierde el juego, llorará. Sí, si perdiera — lloraría. 21) Sí, si su
marido la critica todo el tiempo, le dejará. Sí, si — criticara — le dejaría.
22) Sí, si puedo dejar a mi marido, lo dejaré. Sí, si pudiera le dejaría. 23) Sí,
si el coche está en rebajas, lo compraré. Sí, si — estuviera — lo compraría.
24) Sí, si quieres quedarte me quedaré contigo. Sí, si quisieras — me quedaría
— . 25) Sí, si hay mucha gente en el cine, iremos de todas formas. Sí, si
hubiera — iríamos — . 26) Sí, si trabajo media jornada, ganaré bastante
dinero. Sí, si trabajara — ganaría — . 27) Sí, si intentamos mucho tendremos
éxito. Sí, si intentáramos — tendríamos — . 28) Sí, si la novela es aburrida,
la leeré de todas formas. Sí, si — fuera — la leería — . 29) Sí, si quieren dejar
a los niños con su suegra, estará de acuerdo con tenerles. Sí, si quisieran —
estaría — . 30) Sí, si su novia le quiere, estará muy feliz. Sí, si — le quisiera,
estaría — .

Lección 23, page 111
1) Yes, I've read this book. I read it in January. 2) I have written three
letters today. 3) I've often been to the States. I went there in May. 4) My
husband has seen this picture twice this month. 5) We have eaten a lot in
this restaurant. 6) We went there last Friday. 7) I have bought several dresses
recently. 8) I bought a coat yesterday. 9) She has often been pregnant.
10) She was pregnant last year. 11) He has helped me a lot. 12) He helped
me above all last month. 13) I have often had to see the doctor recently.
14) I had to see the doctor last week. 15) My husband has often travelled.
16) He went to China last year.

Lección 23, page 112
1) Have you guessed the answer yet? 2) Have you beaten your wife already?
3) My husband hasn't yet called me. 4) Has the manager come yet? No, not
yet. 5) Have you ever been to Spain? Yes, twice already. 6) Have you
already met an interesting guy? No, not yet.

Lección 23, page 112
1) ¿Hemos hecho progresos en español ya? Sí, ya hemos hecho progresos.
No, no hemos hecho progresos todavía. 2) ¿Ha ganado mucho dinero ya?
Sí, ya ha ganado mucho dinero. No, no ha ganado mucho dinero todavía.

3) ¿Estás harta ya? Sí, ya estoy harta. No, no estoy harta todavía. 4) ¿Ha encontrado a una chica interesante ya? Sí, ya he encontrado — . No, todavía ne he encontrado — . 5) ¿Ha visitado a su suegra ya? Sí, ya he visitado — . No, todavía no he visitado — . 6) ¿Ha dejado su trabajo ya? Sí, ya ha dejado su trabajo. No, no ha dejado su trabajo todavía. 7) ¿Ha vendido su coche ya? Sí, ha vendido su coche ya. No, no ha vendido su coche todavía. 8) ¿Ha tomado su desayuno ya? Sí, ya ha tomado su desayuno. No, todavía no ha tomado su desayuno. 9) ¿Ha tomado su baño ya? Sí, ya ha tomado su baño. No, no ha — todavía. 10) ¿Cogiste un catarro este invierno ya? Sí, ya he cogido un catarro. No, no he cogido — todavía. 11) ¿Han comido ya, chicos? Sí, ya hemos comido. No, todavía no hemos comido. 12) ¿Ha aprendido otro idioma ya? Sí, ya he aprendido otro idioma. No, no he aprendido otro idioma todavía. 13) ¿Has encontrado tu monedero ya? Sí, ya he encontrado mi monedero. No, todavía no he encontrado mi monedero. 14) ¿Ha hecho su maleta ya? Sí, ya ha hecho su maleta. No, todavía no ha hecho su maleta.

Lección 23, page 113
1) Ví la película la semana pasada. 2) ¿Ha visto esa película? 3) ¿Ha ido alguna vez a Nueva York? 4) Tomó el avión para Madrid la semana pasada. 5) Fumé demasiado anoche. 6) ¿Ha hablado con él hoy? 7) Hablé con él hace unos días. 8) Piensa que ya ha estado casado dos veces. 9) He visto esa película dos veces. 10) La ví por la primera vez el año pasado. 11) Empezamos a estudiar inglés hace un mes. 12) Hemos aprendido mucho en esta clase. 13) No ha visto a su abuela todavía. 14) Hemos ido a Italia muchas veces. 15) Te ha llamado dos veces hoy. 16) La última vez fue hace una hora. 17) Su amigo vino hace poco y salieron juntos hace cinco minutos. 18) Hemos preguntado muchas cosas al profesor en esta clase. 19) Hizo frío ayer. 20) Ha llovido a menudo este invierno. 21) Mi hermano vivió en Nueva York el año pasado. Ha vivido en varios estados en Estados Unidos. 22) Compré esta casa en 1975 y viví allí durante cinco años. 23) Antes de venir a Francia, trabajé como secretaria. 24) También he trabajado en muchos otros trabajos. 25) Necesité ayuda la semana pasada pero esta semana todavía no he necesitado ninguna. 26) Me dió un regalo para mi cumpleaños. 27) Trabajó aquí durante diez años. 28) Le he visto muchas veces desde su accidente. En efecto, le ví ayer.

Lección 24, page 118
1) He has just gone out. 2) Are they still on strike? No, not any more. 3) They still love each other and us too. 4) Do you like coffee? No, I don't like it. 5) Do you have some money? Yes, I have some. 6) We speak only Spanish here. 7) Does it still hurt? No, no more. 8) Do they like chicken? No, they don't like it. 9) We've just finished this work. 10) I'm going to finish another one. 11) Are they still married? No, not any more. 12) Does it still bother you? Yes, it still bothers me. 13) Are they still working part-time? No, not any more. 14) Do you think that he's still sick?

Lección 24, page 118
1) ¿Están casados todavía? No, ya no. 2) ¿Se habla inglés aquí? 3) ¿Tiene azúcar? No, no tengo (nada de) azúcar. 4) ¿Le gustan las legumbres? Sí, me gustan mucho. 5) ¿Riñen todavía mucho? No, ya no. 6) ¿Vd. va a ir esta noche con ella? 7) Acaba de salir hace poco. 8) ¿Está Vd. cansado todavía? No, ya no estoy cansado. 9) ¿Les gusta el pescado? No, no les gusta. 10) ¿Sabe Vd. conducir? 11) Voy a hacer huelga. 12) Acaban de salir. 13) ¿Le gusta a Vd. ganar dinero todavía? Sí, me gusta mucho ganar dinero todavía. 14) Se come mucho pescado en España.

Lección 24, page 119
1) Hace una hora que miró la tele. Miró la tele desde hace une hora. Estoy mirando la tele desde hace una hora. 2) Hace cinco años que viven en Madrid. Viven en Madrid desde hace cinco años. Están viviendo en Madrid desde hace cinco años. 3) Hace dos horas que los niños juegan. Los niños juegan desde hace dos horas. Los niños están jugando desde hace dos horas. 4) Hace doce años que trabaja en esta compañía. Trabaja en esta compañía desde hace doce años. Esta trabajando en esta compañía desde hace doce años. 5) Hace diez horas que duerme. Duerme desde hace diez horas. Está durmiendo desde hace diez horas. 6) Hace dos años que tomamos clases de español. Tomamos clases de español desde hace dos años. Estamos tomando clases de español desde hace dos años. 7) Hace una hora que comemos. Comemos desde hace una hora. Estamos comiendo desde hace una hora. 8) Hace media hora que riñen. Riñen desde hace media hora. Está riñendo desde hace media hora. 9) Hace demasiado tiempo que me fastidias. Me fastidias desde hace demasiado tiempo. Estás fastidiándome desde hace demasiado tiempo. 10) Hace una hora que ando. Ando desde hace una hora. Estoy andando desde hace una hora. 11) Nos enseña español desde hace muchos meses. Hace muchos meses que nos enseña español. Esta enseñándonos español desde hace muchos meses. 12) Bebemos mucho desde nuestro casamiento. 13) Me mientes desde ayer. 14) Hace horas que busco mi bolso. Busco mi bolso desde hace horas. Estoy buscando mi bolso desde hace horas. 15) Me critica desde el principio. 16) Estoy pagando demasiado desde el principio. 17) Está de viaje desde enero. Esta haciendo un viaje desde enero. 18) Los niños lloran desde esta mañana. Los niños estan llorando desde esta mañana.

Lección 25, page 122
1) It's not what you think. 2) It's not what I want to say. 3) I don't understand what you want. 4) I know what they told you. 5) I don't know what to say. 6) What I need is a lot of money.

Lección 25, page 122
1) ¿Sabes lo que quiero comer? 2) Sabemos lo que tenemos que hacer. 3) Eso es lo que me preocupa. 4) ¿Sabe Vd. lo que piensa? 5) Lo que me interesa es poder ir ahora. 6) Eso es lo que quiere decir. 7) Lo que sé es que

Vd. está equivocado. 8) Pienso que es lo que quiere. 9) Lo que le hace falta es un novio simpático. 10) No puedo hacer lo que quieres. 11) No sabrá que hacer. 12) Lo que tiene que hacer es acabar el trabajo inmediatamente.

Lección 25, page 124
1) Had you noticed he needed more money? 2) He went out without paying. 3) The man whose wife died not long ago is my brother. 4) I'm not used to drinking a lot in the afternoon. 5) The writer whose novel was successful is here. 6) Instead of talking we are going to do something. 7) The children whose toys are on the floor are mine. 8) I want to eat it before and not after I go. 9) The cops are not used to killing the gangsters. 10) You need today's newspapers.

Lección25, page 124
1) Los gangsters salieron sin robar nada. 2) El hampa está acostumbrado a tomar drogas. 3) La mujer cuyo marido murió la semana pasada es famosa. 4) ¿En vez de comer ahora, quiere ir a verle al hospital? 5) ¿Te hace falta dinero? 6) Los niños cuyos padres se han divorciado a menudo tienen más éxito más tarde. 7) Al entrar, le ví hablar con otra tía. 8) No estamos acostumbrados a morir antes que nuestros padres. 9) El periodista cuyo libro era un fracaso es un amigo mío. 10) Sin decir nada, le pegó. 11) ¿Le molesta si no estoy acostumbrado a ese tipo de respuesta? 12) En vez de reñir explícame lo que quieres.

Lección 26, page 131
1) Si tuviera éxito, tendría — . Si hubiera tendio — hubiera tenido — . 2) Si pudieras — estaría — . Si hubieras podido — , hubiera estado — . 3) Si le dieran — estaría — . Si hubieran dado — hubiera estado — . 4) Si hubiera que hacerlo, te ayudaría. Si hubiera habido — te hubiera ayudado. 5) Si lloviera, no iríamos. Si hubiera llovido, no hubiéramos ido. 6) Si no me prestara — , no podría — . Si no hubiera prestado — , no hubiera podido — . 7) Si no tuviera que — , jugaría — . Si no hubiera tenido que — , hubiera jugado — . 8) Si pudiera — , tomaría — . Si hubiera podido — , hubiera tomado — . 9) Si tuviera — , encontraría — . Si hubiera tenido — , hubiera encontrado — . 10) Si supiera que — , vendría — . Si hubiera sabido — , hubiera venido — . 11) Si te pareciera — , haría — . Si te hubiera parecido — hubiera hecho — . 12) Si — fuese — , no trabajaría — . Si — hubiera sido — , no hubiera trabajado — . 13) Si hubiera que — , — haría — . Si hubiera habido que — , — hubiera hecho — . 14) Si pudiera venir, vendrías — . Si hubiera podido venir, hubieras venido. 15) Si no supiera que — , se lo dirías? Si hubiera sabido que — , se lo hubieras dicho. 16) Si me desilusionaras, estaría — . Si me hubieras desilusionado, hubiera estado. 17) Si no tuviera — , no te pediría — . Si no hubiera tenido — , no te hubiera pedido — . 18) Si no hicieras — , el profesor te dejaría. Si no hubieras hecho — , el profesor te hubiera dejado. 19) Si no entendieras, te explicaría. Si no hubieras entendido, no te hubiera explicado.

20) Si tuvieras suerte, estaría — . Si hubieras tenido suerte, hubiera estado — .
21) Si te hiciera daño, no seguiría — . Si te hubiera hecho daño, no hubiera
seguido — . 22) Si el zoo estuviera abierto, iríamos — . Si el zoo hubiera
estado abierto, hubiéramos ido — . 23) Si necesitaras — , sabría donde — .
Si hubieras necesitado — , hubiera sabido. 24) Si algo fuera al revés, moriría.
Si hubiera ido al revés, hubiera muerto. 25) Si quisieras, podríamos — . Si
hubieras querido, hubiéramos podido — . 26) Si robaras, — no irías — . Si
hubieras robado. — no hubieras ido — . 27) Si le hicieras — , — te detendrían.
Si le hubieras hecho — , — te hubieran detenido. 28) Si no adelgazaras, — te
dejaría. Si no hubieras adelgazado, — te hubiera dejado.

Lección 26, page 132

1) Si acabas el trabajo hoy, iremos de compras. Si acabaras — iríamos — . Si
hubieras acabado — hubiéramos ido — . 2) Si la película no tiene éxito, no
iré. Si — no tuviera — , no iría. Si — no hubiera tenido — , no hubiera ido.
3) Si el escritor es malo, no leerán sus libros. Si — fuera malo, no leerían —
Si — hubiera sido, no hubieran leído — . 4) Si adelgazas, tu marido estará
feliz. Si adelgazaras, — estaría — . Si hubieras adelgazado, — hubiera estado
— . 5) Si muere, estaré muy triste. Si muriera, estaría — . Si hubiera muerto,
hubiera estado — . 6) ¿Si tengo que ir, vendrás conmigo? ¿Si tuviera que — ,
vendrías — ? ¿Si hubiera tenido que — , hubieras venido — ? 7) Si puede
ayudarte, sé que lo hará. Si pudiera — , lo haría. Si hubiera podido — lo
hubiera hecho. 8) Si la policía coge al asesino, irá preso. Si — cogiera — , iría
— . Si — hubiera cogido — , hubiera ido — . 9) Si el político es honrado, nos
sorprenderá. Si — fuese honrado, nos sorprendería. Si — hubiera sido honrado,
nos hubiera sorprendido. 10) Si el periodista tiene que dar un soborno, dará
uno importante. Si — tuviera — , daría — . Si hubiera tenido — , hubiera dado
— . 11) Si el gangster roba mucho dinero, encontrará a un político para
protegerle. Si — robara — , encontraría — . Si — hubiera robado — , hubiera
encontrado — . 12) Si todo va mal, iré a la cama. Si — fuera — , iría — . Si —
hubiera ido — , hubiera ido — . 13) Si no puede venir, llamará. Si no pudiera
venir, llamaría. Si no hubiera podido venir, hubiera llamado. 14) Si tienen
que pagar la cuenta otra vez, estarán furiosos. Si tuvieran que — , estarían —
Si hubieran tenido que — , hubieran estado — . 15) Si mientes otra vez, estaré
harto. Si mintieras — , estaría — . Si hubieras mentido — , hubiera estado — .
16) Si puedes adivinar, será sorprendente. Si pudieras — , sería — . Si
hubieras podido — , hubiera sido — . 17) Si está encinta, no será con su
marido. Si estuviera — , no sería — . Si hubiera estado — , no hubiera sido — .
18) Si sigues chillando, colgaré. Si siguieras — , colgaría. Si hubieras seguido
— , hubiera colgado. 19) Si me desilusionas otra vez, tendré que dejarte. Si
me desilusionaras, tendría que — . Si me hubieras desilusionado, hubiera
tenido que — . 20) Si gano mucho dinero me casaré con él. Si ganara — me
casaría — . Si hubiera ganado — me hubiera casado — . 21) Si decides ahora,
puedes venir con nosotros. Si decidieras — , podrías — . Si hubieras decidido
— hubieras podido. 22) Si planeas venir, debes decírnoslo. Si planearas — ,

deberías — . Si hubieras planeado — , deberías habérnoslo dicho. 23) Si quieres tomar tu avión, tendrás que hacer tu maleta ahora. Si quisieras — , tendrías — . Si hubieras querido — , hubieras tenido — ; 24) Si te duele la cabeza, podrás descansar. Si te doliera — , podrías — . Si te hubiera dolido — , hubieras podido — . 25) ¿Si un asesinato ocurre en su casa, estará preocupado? ¿Si — ocurriera — , estaría — . ¿Si — hubiera ocurrido — , hubiera estado — . 26) ¿Si no podemos llamarle, entenderá? ¿Si no pudiéramos — , entendería? ¿Si no hubiéramos podido — , hubiera entendido? 27) ¿Si ganamos, tendremos mucho dinero? ¿Si ganáramos, tendríamos mucho dinero? ¿Si hubiéramos ganado, hubiéramos tenido mucho dinero? 28) ¿Si los niños no quieren, irán al zoológico de todas maneras? ¿Si — quisieran, irían — ? ¿Si — hubieran querido, hubieran ido — ?

Lección 27, page 136
1) He should have worked more rapidly. 2) She's not ill any more. He must be a good doctor. 3) He should have said it before. 4) I don't have to go now. 5) We have to go tomorrow. 6) You shouldn't have talked to her like that. 7) The coat was cheap. They must have lowered the prices. 8) We have to take the plane to go to Madrid. 9) I can't find my umbrella. I must have lost it. 10) We must call her anyway. 11) You should eat instead of talking so much. 12) I must post the letter right now. 13) Did he have to retire last year? 14) He didn't answer. He can't have understood.

Lección 27, page 136
1) Se supone que tengo que ir esta noche. 2) ¿Tenemos que pagar mucho dinero por la casa? 3) ¿Debería un asesino ir a la cárcel? 4) Debería llamarla esta noche, pero no lo haré. 5) ¿Tienes que trabajar este fin de semana? 6) ¿Por qué hicieron eso? Deben ser locos. 7) Tengo que hablarle. 8) ¿Debería comprarle un regalo para sus cumpleaños? 9) Los hombres no vinieron. Los sindicatos deben hacer huelga. 10) El jefe no está. Debe estar enfermo. 11) No tenemos que trabajar esta noche. 12) A mi parecer debería Vd. aceptar lo que hace. 13) Tengo que admitir que tiene razón. 14) No debería pegar a su mujer.

Lección 28, page 138
1) Her boyfriend is so amusing that she never gets bored. 2) The boss was so cross that he went out. 3) You talk so much! 4) He eats so much that he puts on a lot of weight. 5) She's so tired that she will stay in bed. 6) We danced so much!

Lección 28, page 138
1) Es tan cabezona que no le escucha nunca. 2) Habla tan francamente que hace daño. 3) ¡Es Vd. tan rico! 4) Bebía tanto café que no podía dormir. 5) ¡Su tío es tan guapo! 6) Están tan infelices que deberían divorciarse.

Lección 28, page 140
1) What do you think of her husband? 2) Do you like the plane? 3) I don't know whether he will come back or not. 4) When will he become rich? 5) I want something to drink, but I don't want coffee. 6) Do they like cakes? 7) Do monkeys like bananas?

Lección 28, page 140
1) ¿Les gustan a los periodistas los viajes? 2) No sabemos si quiere venir o no. 3) Me parece bien si vamos ahora. 4) ¿Le encanta a Vd. la idea? 5) No es realmente una puta sino una mujer libre. 6) ¿Sabe Vd. si está de acuerdo o no? 7) Les encanta bailar pero por otra parte no les gustan las danzas modernas.

Lección 29, page 144
1) Is this car even more expensive than the other one? Yes that one is even more expensive. 2) Do you mind working abroad? 3) Yes, I do because it is even more difficult. 4) There were many passengers delighted with the trip. 5) Can you bring me a glass, please? 6) I don't know how to drive a car, on the other hand I know how to ride a horse. 7) Can I take her with me tonight? 8) Do you mind our eating together in this quiet place? 9) I'll come back later and then I will call you again. 10) I want one tea. 11) I love my husband more than my kids. 12) Is this guy more of an ass than the other? Yes, he's even more stupid. 13) Do you mind going right now? 14) Even though I'm tired I'm going to dance.

Lección 29, page 144
1) Vamos a hacer el trabajo otra vez. 2) ¿Le quiere? 3) Puede llevarle con Vd. si quiere. 4) Había mucha gente en el cine. 5) ¿Es esta cosa aún más cara que la otra? 6) No importa. 7) La cosa es que aunque conduzco no quiero tomar mi coche. 8) Incluso los pasajeros tuvieron miedo. 9) Habrá mucha gente en la casa. 10) El propietario lleva a su hermano 11) ¿Les importa trabajar por la noche? 12) El hampa va a intentar matarle otra vez. 13) ¿Le gusta mucho el dinero? 14) Si, pero aún así no mataría por dinero.

Lección 30, page 148
1) He is often wrong. 2) He remembers his last vacation. 3) Is your name Perez? 4) I'm getting bored by what he says. 5) Does he often complain? 6) They are going to be divorced this year. 7) Are you going to get married next month? 8) Do you undress in front of your husband? 9) Do you sometimes go for a walk at weekends? 10) Do you get up early every morning? 11) They enjoy themselves a lot in the evening. 12) How do you feel? 13) We felt cold a lot this winter. 14) Your father never gets angry with your brothers.

Lección 30, page 148

1) Estoy lavándome y visitiéndome y lista para la fiesta. 2) Nos preguntamos adonde querías ir. 3) Se hará médico pronto. 4) Nos divertiremos mucho esta noche. 5) Me equivoco todo el tiempo. 6) ¿Te das cuenta de lo que dices? 7) Si te apetece, iremos a pasearnos. 8) Si no te acuestas temprano, no te levantarás nunca a tiempo. 9) ¿Por qué no te pones un abrigo? 10) No me acuerdo de su cara. 11) Se queja siempre. 12) No puedo acostumbrarme a lo que fuma. 13) No me importa lo que Vd. dice. 14) Vamos de prisa, llevamos retraso.

Lección 31, page 150

1) él mismo 2) tú misma 3) Vd. mismo 4) él mismo 5) mismos 6) él mismo
7) mismos 8) él mismo 9) ella misma 10) ella misma

Lección 31, page 151

1) Vd. se puso nervioso ayer, y se ha puesto nervioso otra vez hoy. Vd. se pone — . 2) No se dió cuenta de que su marido le mentía. No se da cuenta — . 3) Las chicas subieron para desvestirse y lavarse. Las chicas suben — . 4) Nos hablábamos cada semana. 5) Nos despertamos tarde de vacaciones y ahora nos despertamos temprano para trabajar. Nos despertamos — . 6) No me equivoqué ayer y no me equivoco ahora. No me equivoco — . 7) ¿A qué hora se acostó ayer? ¿A qué hora se acuesta esta noche? 8) No me acordé de su marido ni de sus hijos. No me acuerdo — . 9) Nos divertimos mucho anoche, y siempre nos divertimos. Nos divertimos — . 10) Me dí prisa pero no se dió cuenta de que quería verle más temprano. Me doy prisa pero no se da cuenta de que — . 11) Volvió a casarse, me pregunto si se acuerda de todos sus maridos. Vuelve a — . 12) El profesor se enfadó y se cansa rápidamente. El profesor se enfada y — . 13) Me quité el abrigo viejo y me puse el nuevo. Me quito el abrigo viejo y me pongo — . 14) Empezamos a trabajar y nos dimos cuenta de lo feliz que nos pusimos al poder hacerlo todo sin una falta. Empezamos a trabajar y nos damos cuenta de lo feliz que nos pone — .

Lección 32, page 155

1) Nos paseamos — . 2) ¿Harás — . La hice — . 3) Mira — . 4) Fuimos — . 5) Leía mientras dormías. 6) Está riñendo — . 7) Ha estado — . 8) Desde cuando está — . 9) Conducía — ocurrió. 10) Están casados — . 11) Duerme — . 12) Cuando la policía llegó los gamberros habían robado — . 13) Pienso que ha salido — . 14) Aprendo — . 15) Has visto — . 16) Tuve que — . 17) Qué hacía Vd. cuando entré. 18) Está infeliz — . 19) Empezaremos — . 20) Puede hacerlo ayer y no podré — . 21) Trato de — . 22) Hacíamos la comida cuando entraron — . 23) Se lavaron esta mañana. Nos lavamos — . 24) Recuerdas lo que decía cuando le encontramos — . 25) Me dice — . 26) Era profesor en Madrid antes de irse — . 27) Se divorciaron hace seis meses. ¿Desde cuando está divorciado? 28) Arreglaremos el coche roto.

Lección 32, page 156

1) Si puedo, iré con Vd. Si pudiera, iría con Vd. Si hubiera podido, hubiera ido. 2) Si no te desvistes, te pegaré. Si no te desvistieras te pegaría. Si no te hubieras desvestido te hubiera pegado. 3) ¿Si se quieren, por qué no se casan? ¿Si se quisieran por qué no se casarían? ¿Si se hubieran querido . . . hubieran casado? 4) Si te enfadas otra vez te dejaré. Si te enfadaras otra vez te dejaría. Si te hubieras enfadado otra vez te hubiera dejado. 5) Si no tenemos que hacer el trabajo ahora, iremos de paseo. Si no tuviéramos que hacer el trabajo ahora, iríamos de paseo. Si no hubiéramos tenido que hacer el trabajo ahora, hubiéramos ido de paseo. 6) Si no trabaja no aprobará su examen. Si no trabajara no aprobaría su examen. Si no hubiera trabajado no hubiera aprobado su examen. 7) Si tienen dinero el año próximo, comprarán otra casa. Si tuvieran dinero el año próximo, comprarían otra casa. Si hubieran tenido dinero el año próximo, hubieran comprado otra casa. 8) Si podemos ayudar, le llamaremos. Si pudiéramos ayudar, le llamaríamos. Si hubiéramos podido ayudar, le hubiéramos llamado. 9) Si no puede vender su coche, se lo compraré. Si no pudiera vender su coche, se lo compraría. Si no hubiera podido vender su coche, se lo hubiera comprado. 10) Si es un tonto su novia no le querrá. Si fuera un tonto su novia no le querría. Si hubiera sido un tonto su novia no le hubiera querido. 11) Si la policía puede prender al gangster, le pondrá en la cárcel. Si la policiá pudiera prender al gangster, le pondría en la cárcel. Si la policía hubiera podido prender al gangster, le hubiera puesto en la cárcel. 12) Si tu hermana toma la píldora no estará encinta. Si tu hermana tomara la píldora no estaría encinta. Si tu hermana hubiera tomado la píldora no hubiera estado encinta. 13) Si quiere abortar el médico lo hará. Si quisiera abortar el medico lo haría. Si hubiera querido abortar el medicolo hubiera hecho. 14) Si los trabajadores se ponen en huelga los sindicatos estarán felices. Si los trabajadores se pusieran en huelga los sindicatos estarían felices. Si los trabajadores se hubieran puesto en huelga los sindicatos hubieran estado felices. 15) Si hay otra guerra moriremos todos. Si hubiera otra guerra moriríamos todos. Si hubiera habido otra guerra hubiéramos muerto todos. 16) Si no te paras de quejarte chillaré. Si no te pararas de quejarte chillaría. Si no te hubieras parado de quejarte hubiera chillado. 17) Si quiere ir de viaje, iré con Vd. Si quisiera ir de viaje, iría con Vd. Si hubiera querido ir de viaje, hubiera ido con Vd. 18) Si los políticos no toman sobornos, será sorprendente. Si los políticos no tomaran sobornos, sería sorprendente. Si los políticos no hubieran tomado sobornos, hubiera sido sorprendente. 19) Si recibimos hoy los impuestos temprano, estaremos en un atolladero. Si recibiéramos hoy los impuestos temprano, estaríamos en un atolladero. Si hubiéramos recibido hoy los impuestos temprano, hubiéramos estado en un atolladero. 20) Si no tomamos la autopista, el viaje será más largo. Si no tomáramos la autopista, el viaje sería más largo. Si no hubiéramos tomado la autopista, el viaje hubiera sido más largo. 21) Si los soldados se niegan a hacer guerra, el mundo estará feliz por fin. Si los soldados se negaran

a hacer guerra, el mundo estaría feliz por fin. Si los soldados se hubieran negado a hacer guerra, el mundo hubiera estado feliz por fin. 22) Si su política es tan tonta, no votaremos por él. Si su política fuese tan tonta, no votaríamos por él. Si su política hubiera sido tan tonta, no hubieramos votado por él. 23) Si tengo que adelgazar haré una dieta. Si tuviera que adelgazar haría una dieta. Si hubiera tenido que adelgazar hubiera hecho una dieta. 24) Si este tío está loco se hará soldado. Si este tío estuviera loco se haría soldado. Si este tío hubiera estado loco, se hubiera hecho soldado. 25) Si le reconoces tendrás suerte. Si le reconocieras, tendrías suerte. Si le hubieras reconocido, hubieras tenido suerte. 26) Si hace mal tiempo, nos quedaremos dentro. Si hiciera mal tiempo, nos quedaríamos dentro. Si hubiera hecho mal tiempo, nos hubiéramos quedado dentro. 27) Si no quieres quedarte aquí sola, te dejaré los niños. Si no quisieras quedarte aquí sola, te dejaría los niños. Si no hubieras querido quedarte aquí sola, te hubiera dejado los niños. 28) Si sigues preocupándote tanto por él, pensaré que le quieres. Si siguieras preocupándote tanto por él, pensaría que le quieres. Si hubieras seguido preocupándote tanto por él, hubiera pensado que le quieres.

Lección 32, page 157
1) Son novios desde Navidad. ¿Te parece que van a casarse pronto? 2) Reía mientras se enfadaba. 3) Debería darle un regalo para sus cumpleaños y debería haberle dado uno el año pasado. 4) Hace dos horas que trato de llamarle. 5) Me preguntaba si iba a venir. 6) No veo a nadie y no oigo nada. 7) No tengo más que un poco de dinero. ¿Me puedes prestar algo? 8) Nuestra firma procura computadoras a la fábrica desde hace años. 9) No entendimos nada. No entiende nunca nada. 10) Me divorciaba cuando le encontré. 11) Intento comprenderle. 12) No tienes que tomar tu propio jabón contigo. 13) ¿Por qué estás tan enfadado? No me quejo. 14) Los gamberros estaban robando el banco cuando la policía llegó. 15) No deberías haber tomado esas drogas. 16) No puedo ayudarle. Estoy demasiado cansado. 17) Pega a su mujer desde que nació su hijo. 18) ¿Hace cuánto tiempo que está encinta? 19) Mi pierna me duele desde mi accidente. 20) ¿Os molesta si fumo mientras coméis? 21) Tuve que dejar una propina. Deberías haber dejado una también. 22) ¿No podría permanecer honrado en política? ¿Y Vd.? 23) El hampa es tan fuerte que todos tenemos miedo. 24) ¿Hace cuánto tiempo que está casado? 25) ¿Sabías que hacía el amor con su secretaria mientras estabas de viaje? 26) Debería haberse acostumbrado a sus bromas hace mucho. 27) Debería haberme dicho antes que no iba a venir. 28) Pagamos impuestos altos y fuimos a la quiebra al mismo tiempo.

Lección 32, page 158
1) Estás haciendo la misma comida desde esta mañana. 2) Es un maricón y su hermana es una puta. 3) ¿Te hace falta ayuda? 4) Mi brazo me ha dolido

todo el día. 5) Voy a lavarme y vestirme y prepararme para salir. 6) Vivió en Nueva York durante diez años cuando era joven y ahora vive en Madrid desde hace dos años. 7) ¿Te das cuenta de lo tontos que son? 8) No me acuerdo de su nombre. Debes preguntárselo. 9) Venden saldos desde Navidad. 10) Estamos haciendo computadoras desde hace mucho. 11) Tengo que decirle algo importante. 12) Intentaba ayudarle pero se enfadó. 13) Debería haber ido conmigo ayer. No me escucha nunca cuando le digo que debería venir conmigo. 14) No tenía que hacerlo hoy. Tengo que hacerlo para mañana. 15) Estaban robando todo cuando llegó la policía. 16) No está aquí. Debe estar enferma. 17) Tiene que dar sobornos si quiere ayuda de los políticos. 18) No pude ir con Vd. ayer, pero hubiera podido ir el día antes. 19) Deberías haber llamado y haberme dicho que estabas en un atolladero. 20) No sabía que hacer, entonces le dijo que debería ver al jefe. 21) Si fueras un amigo suyo, estarías acostumbrado a beber mucho también. 22) ¡Qué primo eres! No deberías haberle creido. 23) No podía verle y no entiendo como le puede querer. 24) Tenías que ser un tonto para creer todo lo que el político dijo. 25) Iba a jubilarse cuando sus niños cayeron enfermos. 26) No tengo que ayudarte como no me has ayudado cuando lo necesitaba. 27) Puede venir si le apetece. No me importa. 28) Me importa un bledo! ¡Puede ir al diablo!